The Astrology of Choice

The Astrology of Choice

A Counseling Approach

Roy Alexander

SAMUEL WEISER, INC.
York Beach, ME 03910

Published in 1983 by
Samuel Weiser, Inc.
P. O. Box 612
York Beach, Maine 03910

Copyright © Roy D. Alexander

ISBN 0-87728-563-2

Library of Congress Cataloging in Publication Data

Alexander, Roy, 1931–
    The astrology of choice.

    1. Astrology.   2. Counseling--Miscellanea.
I. Title.
BF1729.C67A4   1983   133.5   83–6486

Typeset by Positive Type
Printed and bound by Maple-Vail

Contents

Give me a place to stand and I will move the world.

Archimedes

Preface

I have called this book *The Astrology of Choice* because it is essentially about choosing the chart that we have instead of being the victim of it. The method I am proposing offers a way of looking at and utilizing astrology that can unblock the processes that we are stuck in, rather than seeing the chart as just another way of finding out how limited we are. Although we may not be conscious of it, we are in a constant process of choosing our chart. It is when we become conscious of this *compulsive* choosing, when we are able to acknowledge that process and take responsibility for it, that we are able to create the space to choose something other than more of what we have had in the past.

The ideas put forward in the first section of the book are presented as a framework for effective counseling. They can, of course, equally well be used for one's own self-counseling. Indeed, if the counseling of clients is to be effective, they need to be more than merely intellectual concepts or beliefs; they need to be experienced as valid in your own life. The experience does not have to be a very big one to begin with. You can start, as I did, with not much more than a glimpse of the truth of these principles; the experience of the truth of them will expand as you use them in your own life and in work with clients. This is no different from any other field. Taking an example near to home, having an intellectual grasp of the principles of astrology and a belief in its validity is not at all the same as interpreting a chart for a real live client. It is only as you gain confidence that astrology really *works* in a practical way that you can become a skilled chart interpreter. In the same way, you need to gain confidence that the counseling principles that I describe really work.

These principles can be summed up briefly. We have problems and our lives are bogged down or in crisis essentially because we are so stuck in a huge mass of beliefs, concepts, assumptions and preconceptions about the way our lives *should* be and the way the world *should* be that we hardly ever have our attention on what actually *is* so. We are unable to trust our own natural knowing and being and to align ourselves with the inherent flow of our lives. Some of these beliefs and assumptions are extremely detrimental to us, yet, at a certain level, we cling to them because we imagine that we need them in order to survive. One can say that these patterns develop in childhood. If our parents are not loving we will adopt the belief that surviving means doing without adequate love. It is not just a matter of having the body survive either. It is more a matter of having a sense of ourselves as lovable and worthy beings survive. Paradoxically, people can kill themselves in order to survive.

These patterns continue to run our lives until we confront them and—most important—until we recognize that it is our own intention, based on mistaken ideas about survival, that keeps them going. If we didn't get adequately loved as children, there wasn't much that we could do about it. We could either go along with the situation or we could die. But we internalize the lack of love—or whatever the childhood situation may be—and we go on making it a basic operating principle of the rest of our lives.

Unblocking our problems, and having them clear up, is essentially a matter of clarifying what we are doing with our life, what is actually so about it, and taking responsibility for it. In a sentence: *Be here now and be responsible for being here now.* In this context, being responsible for our problems means reclaiming and reowning the intention we put into them in the first place.

Where the traumas come from is less important than the fact that they exist and one's willingness to look at them clearly. Analysis of parent-child relationships is frequently useful, and I have devoted a chapter to a consideration of how destructive patterns arise. The real value of such analysis, however, is not in discovering the "origin" of a problem but in getting clear about what the problem is. In childhood, the issues are there in a stark and simple way. As we grow up, we bury them and cover them over with so many other things that we often cannot see them clearly. Sometimes the only way to have a person see what is so about himself *now* is to have him look at what *was* so about himself when he was a child. But the goal is really to get him to own and accept the destructive patterns that are running his life *now*. We have to move on from putting the responsibility for being the way we are onto our parents, no matter how awful they were. And, for that matter, no matter how wonderful they were.

Analysis and pushing the problem further back in time in the search for a definite origin of it does not, of itself, do anything to clear up the problem. What does clear the problem up is the nonjudgmental acceptance of and assumption of responsibility for what is actually so about us. The big problem is that what is actually so about us is hard to see because of our preconceptions and beliefs. We have to go to somebody who can hold up an accurate reflection of ourselves to us. Holding up such a mirror is what I basically see as my function and the function of astrology.

The reader accustomed to the format of most books on astrology will no doubt find the material in this one unfamiliar at first. He or she may be surprised to find comparatively little emphasis on astrology as such, especially in the example counseling sessions. The reason is that, although I have included some guidelines to interpretation in Section 2, the book is primarily about the *use* of the chart information, not the extraction of it. Most books treat interpretation of the chart as an end in itself. In this one it is only a means to an end—and that end is empowering a client to live a more productive and fulfilling life, or at least to move toward doing so.

Just interpreting the chart is not, in itself, empowering to the client. Yet, at present, by far the main effort of astrologers as a whole is focused on chart interpretation. Our current technology for extracting information from the birth chart is impressive and, to a large degree, reliable. Nevertheless, as astrologers, we remain defensive about our subject. There is a strong feeling among many of us that we have to prove astrology and make it acceptable to scientific opinion. Much of the present enthusiasm for computer studies has its origin in such feelings.

However, I suggest that our defensiveness about astrology does not spring from doubts about its scientific validity, but rather from our misgivings about its practical usefulness. It arises because we have so little idea of what to do with the information that we derive from our charts. A technology for using such information, comparable to the technology for extracting it, hardly exists. It is a major purpose of this book to lay the foundations of such a technology. It is time for astrology to move on from an introverted obsession with interpretation techniques and to start to be truly effective in the world.

I don't intend to diminish the importance of interpretation. In fact, the better you are at chart interpretation the better you are going to be able to do the counseling part of the session. Having accurate information to begin with is a cornerstone of the method of counseling that I describe. It is my preference now to begin a session with a client with a full set of written notes on the chart and a list of the half dozen or so main chart themes, prepared well ahead of time. I have the chart on hand during the interview, but I often don't even look at it, let alone use any astrological terminology. The chart has done its job before the session begins, and my attention can be focused on using the information obtained from it to get a result.

It will be evident that the counseling method used does not depend specifically on the chart as a source of information. The method can equally well be used with, say, tarot, a Rorschach test, dream analysis or just plain talking to the person. Anything that will provide a useable piece of information about the client's psychological structures will suffice. However, it seems clear to me that the astrological chart is far and away the most effective, comprehensive and reliable source of information about the client. I take it for granted that astrology works, and that we have enough cumulative experience to know that it works, whether the computer studies and the scientists agree with us or not.

But there is more to it than the chart being such a powerful source of information. My assumption is that each person is literally the center of his own universe. That universe has distinctive qualities, and the chart is a coded summary of these qualities. Using the birth chart to have the client become clear about and responsible for those distinctive qualities actually realigns him with his own universe. The use of astrology is therefore totally appropriate to this work.

Everyone who has ever had any personal contact with me, however brief, has made a contribution to my life and, therefore, to this book, and I am glad to acknowledge it. There are some people I specifically want to name, because their ideas have been major influences on my thinking. On the astrological side, I am especially indebted to the writings of Dane Rudhyar, Stephen Arroyo, Reinhold Ebertin, Joanne Wickenburg, Marc Robertson and Zip Dobyns. On the counseling side, I have in the body of the book acknowledged the influence of Eric Berne's Transactional Analysis. Other major influences are Fritz Perls' Gestalt Therapy and Roberto Assagioli's Psychosynthesis. A special acknowledgment is due to Werner Erhard, the founder of the *est* training. Much of the clarity that I have about the processes described in the book has its origin in his clarity.

Finally, I need to acknowledge my clients, the people who were willing to go through this process of self-discovery with me—with particular thanks to the pseudonymous Martin, Peter and Barbara, who have generously shared their sessions as example material.

Roy Alexander
February 1983

PART
I

Rethinking
the Role of Astrology

1

Turning Information Into Knowledge

This book is about having astrology be truly effective in people's lives. To this end we need to look at what it is that is effective, that enables people to move on from being stuck in their problems, and to open up new and more satisfying avenues of self-expression.

There's no big mystery about what this empowering factor is. It is knowledge—specifically, self-knowledge. But, and it is a big *but*, we need to become very clear about what knowledge is and what it consists of Most of the time we confuse knowledge with information. Knowledge is empowering, but information isn't. Information may be interesting, fascinating, reassuring, ego-building, or it may, of course, be depressing and discouraging—but it is not empowering. Knowledge always puts you in a position to make a shift in your life. You may or may not like it, but it empowers you.

The concern of this book is with astrology as a healing system, as a psychological tool. It is not concerned with predicting events, or with good and bad days for doing things. The focus will be on astrological counseling, and especially on the metaphysical background or context that is necessary for counseling to be truly effective. Obviously, chart interpretation is important and will be considered in the second section, but interpretation is not the primary focus of this book. There are many excellent books and courses on interpretation, and I assume that the reader knows at least the basics. The focus here is what to do with the interpretation when it has been made: How can you, or your clients, actually use the interpretation so as to make a shift in your lives? How are we to go about turning information into knowledge?

There seems to be a growing unease among astrologers as to how useful astrology is. It is a common experience for an astrologer to do an accurate and penetrating character analysis for a client, and to have the analysis enthusiastically accepted only to find that it makes little real difference and that the client remains stuck in the same problems. There is little doubt that astrology works, in the sense that the chart can provide an accurate personality assessment, but what's the point of it?

In recent years this issue has led concerned astrologers to investigate various systems of psychology and psychotherapy in an attempt to extend their understanding of astrological symbols. The idea behind doing this has been to enable them to get a deeper interpretation of the chart, to uncover the deeper roots of a client's difficulties. Just about every workable system of psychology has been investigated: Freud, Jung, Reich, Transactional Analysis, Gestalt, Psychosynthesis, are among those that have made valuable contributions. As a result, our understanding of astrological symbolism has moved a long way from the fatalistic, fortune-telling interpretations that were all that was available at the beginning of the 20th century. An astrologer who wants to do so can now, with some confidence, lead a client beyond the more obvious manifestations of the chart to their probable origin in childhood pressures.

The scope of the information that we, as astrologers, are able to give our clients has certainly been extended, but it still doesn't empower them to change their lives. The underlying assumption of "deeper is better" that seemed so promising a few years ago has turned out to be rather disappointing in terms of practical results.

If we have a client with, for example, Moon square Saturn, who is manifesting shyness and emotional inhibition, it does seem likely that it will enable him to get a better handle on the emotional inhibition if we can refer it back to insufficient love and attention from his parents in very early childhood. If the client is at all willing to look at these patterns, he may, in the course of the session, get in touch with the mechanism of inhibition as it developed in response to his parents' behavior. He winds up with more information about himself, but he is still shy and emotionally inhibited. In fact, he may now feel that he has even better reasons for being the way he is.

The idea of "get to the cause and then we'll be able to fix it" is a carry-over from the way we have learned to deal with the physical world. If a piece of machinery fails to function, there is a well-established procedure for tracing the trouble back to its origin in a faulty part and then fixing the damaged component. When we try to apply this procedure to emotional malfunctioning it doesn't work. For one thing, where is the "cause" of an emotional malfunction? In childhood? At birth? In the womb? In a past life? It's always possible to find some earlier trauma. Even if we found the cause, what's the equivalent of replacing the damaged component? As we shall see, it is our mechanical ideas of cause and effect and of space and time that are at the root of the difficulty.

At the time of this writing (1981) there is a loud cry among astrologers of "we need more research." There seems to be a feeling, not very well articulated, that if we can only run more and better computer studies we will have some really hard facts about how astrology works and then we can make it *really* effective. The fallacy again lies in the assumption that astrology works in terms of mechanical cause and effect. It is an extremely unlikely assumption, given the nature of the subject— no one has yet come up with an even halfway plausible theory to account for the seeming effect of the planets—yet, we are all so hypnotized by this so-called scientific way of looking at things that we automatically fall into it.

New data, whether it be from depth psychology or from research, is always welcome, but the truth is that we already have as much data as we need in order to use astrology as a complete healing system. As I have suggested, the problem is that we don't know how to use the data.

The reason for the failure of astrology, as at present generally practiced, to make as much difference in people's lives as it has the potential to do, is that it gets stuck at the level of being information. What turns information into knowledge is experience, the client's experience. There is much talk in astrological circles about synthesizing a chart, but the only way and the only place a chart gets synthesized is when the information becomes a living reality for the client. It sounds very simple and obvious when stated like that, but simple is not the same thing as easy. The reason that it is not easy is that we all have a very large investment in staying unconscious of what is actually going on in our experience. Our daily lives consist of a great deal of hiding, avoiding and downright lying to ourselves in order to conform to our images of the way things should be rather than recognizing the way they are. In a very real sense, all we need to do is to acknowledge and accept, without judgments, what is actually so about ourselves. Until we do that, we are stuck in the lies and evasions.

Jung puts it very neatly: "We must be able to let things happen in the psyche. For us, this is an art of which most people know nothing. Consciousness is forever interfering, helping, correcting and negating, never leaving the psychic processes to grow in peace. It would be simple enough, if only simplicity were not the most difficult of all things." And again, "The most beautiful truth...is no use at all unless it has become the innermost experience and possession of the individual....The needful thing is not to *know* the truth but to *experience* it. Not to have an intellectual conception of things, but to find our way to the inner, and perhaps wordless, irrational experience—that is the great problem."* (Original italics.)

When Jung talks about *knowing* the truth, he is using the word in the sense in which I am using the expression "having information"—it is head knowledge, not experience. I am using the word "know" in the same sense as it is used in the famous statement in the Bible, "You shall know the truth and the truth shall make you free." St. John 8:32.** This does not mean, "There is some big secret, and when you finally get to know it everything will be wonderful." It means, "When you truly experience, accept and take responsibility for being the way you are, you will no longer be stuck in the problem—you will be free of it." Interpreted this way, it isn't a promise, it's an instruction—an instruction on how to get enlightened and liberated. Moreover, it is an instruction that we can carry out literally every minute of the day.

We need to look more closely at the meaning of the word "experience" as it is used in this context. I will define "experience" as the sum total of the sights, sounds, smells, body sensations, emotions, images, thoughts and intuitions that are going on with you now. All that life is really about is experiencing what you are experiencing, when you are experiencing it. Ordinary as this may sound, it is the key to clearing up the problems and situations that we are stuck in. In fact, this ordinary, everyday experience is the philosopher's stone that the alchemists wrote about. (The philosopher's stone was the substance that was said to transmute base metals into gold. It was described as a common substance that could be found anywhere and everywhere, even in filth, but its value went unrecognised.)

The only point at which we have power, at which we can be healed, is in the now. Fritz Perls, the founder of Gestalt Therapy, talked about the "awareness continuum," meaning a technique of becoming fully aware of each actual experience, and therefore staying in touch with the

---

*C.G. Jung, *Psychological Reflections*, 2nd Edition, London: Routledge & Kegan Paul, 1971; C. G. Jung, *Psychological Reflections: A New Anthology of His Writings, 1905-1961*, ed. Jolande Jacobi and R. F. C. Hull, Bolligen Series XXXI. Copyright 1953 by Princeton University Press. Excerpts, pp. 298, 299, reprinted by permission of Princeton University Press.

**The New English Bible*, OUP, CUP, 1970, New Test., p. 123.

experience of being in the "now." It is something that is extremely difficult to do because we are full of theories, explanations, justifications and belief systems about the way things *should* be. Moreover, if we stay aware of what we are experiencing, moment to moment, we frequently get into an experience that is unpleasant. In fact, since life always consists of those experiences that we call "pleasant" and those we call "unpleasant," staying with the flow of things will inevitably lead to something unpleasant. It may manifest as simply feeling bored with the exercise, or feelings of anger may come up, or sadness, for example. At this point, we usually interrupt the process. We may block the feeling, and go unconscious of it, or we may start explaining it and justifying it to ourselves. We may remember that there is something important to be done, or we may go off into a rambling free association of ideas. Whatever we do, we abort the awareness of what we are actually experiencing. Having got our hands on the philosopher's stone that can turn the base metal of our lives into gold, we throw it away because we don't like the way it looks! To put it in a nutshell, we rarely actually align ourselves with the way things are.

One reason that we don't like to align ourselves with the way things are is that we believe that the way things are is a fixed state. There is a fear that, if I experience my anger, I am going to discover that there is nothing but anger in my universe and I am stuck with it for ever and ever. Or whatever other condition I am afraid to be fully aware of. It does not necessarily have to be a negative condition. A lot of people are just afraid to experience happiness or love or excitement.

To overcome this fear, we need to realize that solid, fixed things and conditions are a creation of the observer, the human mind. If, by paying attention to our experience, we get in touch with the experience of the NOW, we discover that this basic experience is that of a very alive no-thing-ness, full of creative potential. The universe is not static. This has been amply demonstrated by modern physics. The ultimate constituents of matter cannot be said to be things at all, in any sense in which we normally use the term. Rather, they are processes.

Perhaps the most fundamental basic law of this universe, and certainly the one that has the biggest and most practical implications for the kind of practice of astrology that I am talking about, is that the universe is essentially a three-stage process. The three stages are creation, maintenance and destruction. The zodiac itself offers a clear and convenient example of this process, which is embodied in the familiar qualities of cardinal, fixed and mutable. A very personally oriented kind of energy is created in Aries, maintained in Taurus and destroyed or dissipated in Gemini. The destruction of that particular kind of energy clears the space for something else to be created. A new type of energy, still personal but more nurturing and aware of others, is then created in Cancer, maintained in Leo and destroyed in Virgo. An energy of one-to-one partnership is created in Libra, maintained in Scorpio and destroyed in Sagittarius. Finally, a collectively oriented energy is created in Capricorn, maintained in Aquarius and destroyed in Pisces.

For those who like to have a nitty-gritty application for everything, I should add that I see no evidence that people with predominantly mutable signs in their charts are any better at confronting their experience and clearing up unfinished business than anyone else. Neverthless, as an abstraction, the example is a valid one. This natural flow to destruction is not so easy to see in human affairs because we so rarely align ourselves with it, and issues get stuck in the maintenance phase.

The cycles of creation, maintenance and destruction are the psychic processes that Jung talks about in the quoted passage. This cycle is the foundation of the healing process in the psyche and *all our problems can be regarded as processes that are stuck in the maintenance phase*. The reason they are stuck is because of our attachment or resistance to them, our unwillingness to be aware of and responsible for our experience of the NOW. All we have to do to have our problems clear up is to tell the truth about them, observe them nonjudgmentally and allow the natural flow of the universe to happen. As Jung says, "It would be simple enough, if only simplicity were not the most difficult of all things."*

The material presented in these last few pages has been intentionally somewhat repetitious. Repetition is a device for getting past the mind's resistance to having its survival beliefs disturbed. This resistance is always very high and can take many forms. To the extent that truth is paradoxical, it is the mind's job in life to resist hearing truth. At least, that's what it conceives its job to be. Later on, we will look at the role of the mind in more detail. For now, let's consider an example of what might happen if someone experiences his experience and turns information into knowledge.

Let's suppose a person, say a student, has difficulty in concentrating. He's bright and intelligent but he gets poor grades because he can hardly sit at his books for more than about ten minutes at a time. Of course, he is going to be well aware of this at the level of information. If he takes the usual, superficial view of it, he accepts it as "just the way he is."

Typically, we might suppose, he settles down for a couple of hours study. During that time, he gets up to make coffee three times, spends

*Supra, p.o.

twenty minutes looking for some notes, feels hungry and has to raid the refrigerator, then, since he's taking a break anyway, calls his girlfriend and talks about how hard it is to get down to work. Probably less than fifty per cent of his allotted study time is spent actually working. And this is with a subject that interests him!

What I want to be very clear about at this point, because it is crucial to understand this, is that the student is not *experiencing* what is going on with him. He is stuck in a concept, a belief system, called "I can't concentrate." He is stuck in the maintenance phase of the process. He doesn't actually observe what is going on and tell the truth to himself about it. He either succumbs to his feelings of unease or resists them by forcing himself to concentrate. Either way, the inability to concentrate persists. He may find ways of working around the difficulty so that he can function. Maybe it helps if he has a couple of drinks before he settles down and has the radio playing while he's working. If the underlying tension is not too severe, he may discover gimmicks that work well enough for the inability to concentrate to cease, apparently, to be a problem.

If, on the other hand, he allows himself to become aware of what is going on with him when he is trying to study—if he pays attention to the actual thoughts, feelings and body sensations that arise—he might discover that the real issue is the fear of the isolation that studying demands. Let us suppose that there is, in fact, a powerful process of fear of being alone that he always manages to keep out of consciousness and which, therefore, is stuck in the maintenance phase. Now that he is aware of the fear, he has other options than repressing it. In fact, if he can confront it and accept it in a nonjudgmental way, he will unblock the create-maintain-destroy process and the fear will clear up. Of course, it is not this easy in practice, for reasons which we will deal with later, but the example is given for the sake of making the point.

Another essential point that the example illustrates is that, in order to handle his problem, the student has *to begin in the middle* because that's where he is. It may well be that, as he becomes aware of his experience, he will become conscious of incidents from the past and that these may add to his awareness of the issue. But, as I have said, the belief that one can go back to some prior cause and fix it is fallacious and, in fact, helps to keep us stuck. The create-maintain-destroy process is irreversible, and we have to align ourselves with it at whatever point we happen to be.

How does astrology fit into this? Let's take the case where, as suggested above, the gimmicks that the student discovers work well enough to override the concentration problem. The wound is still there, but the scar tissue covers it so effectively that he is hardly aware of it. He passes his examinations and is launched on his career. A few years later, he decides to consult an astrologer about a seemingly unrelated problem, perhaps difficulties in his marriage.

Poor concentration and the fear of being alone will be indicated in the chart in a number of ways. For the sake of argument, let's say that there is Mercury conjunct Uranus and square Neptune, and Moon opposition Saturn. It might very well be that the client is not willing or able to discuss the alienation feelings suggested by the Moon opposition Saturn. With an eye on the Mercury, however, the astrologer can ask about problems of concentration, which will seem less threatening to the client. With a little probing and skillful questioning, the astrologer may then be able to encourage the client to begin to look at the issues underlying the concentration problem and which will be connected with the difficulties in the marriage.

Obviously, this is grossly oversimplified and we will put some flesh on the bare bones of this hypothetical example later on in Chapter 9. It is worth noting, though, at this point, what a fantastic advantage the astrologer has over any other type of counselor or therapist. He has *all* the client's issues laid out before him in the chart. If the client doesn't respond to one, he will respond to another, and without having to perhaps take several sessions groping around to find out what the issues are.

This process of experiencing the issue and moving it back to levels of greater truth is a very natural one. It does not depend on complex psychological theories nor does it require any special training—except in the sense that we all need training in the process of being honest with ourselves and in recognizing the enormous resistance we have to being honest.

Clearly, the astrologer-client relationship that I have hinted at is very different from the one that exists in most consulting sessions as they are currently practiced. To move the practice of astrological counseling to a new level does not require any change in the way charts are interpreted. It does require a change in the way in which the astrologer relates to the client. It means being willing to encounter the client on a basis of equality and to abandon the authoritarian, doctor-patient model. For many astrologers, that itself is a big confrontation, since they feel that they have to impress the client with the accuracy of their interpretations and that they have to keep talking all the time in order to justify their fee.

Even though they might call themselves counselors, most astrologers are information dealers and the way they operate is not very different from the way an expert consultant such as an investment analyst works. Basically, they are coming from the position that their job begins and ends with giving accurate information and they do not consider it their responsibility to be concerned with what use the client is able to make of the information. It has to be said, of course, that this is what a large number, probably the majority, of clients expect and want. Very likely the average client would not welcome being invited to get in touch with his or her experience. Many clients come for reassurance rather than being thrown back on their own resources.

However, there are clients who want more from an astrologer. In my own practice around fifty per cent have had some kind of a chart reading before. They already have accurate information about themselves, but they need support in turning the information into knowledge. As astrologers, we need to equip ourselves to give a service to this type of client. In the next chapter, we will continue to develop a metaphysical framework that will enable us to do this.

2

The Nature of Reality
or: The Monkey and the Nuts

There is an aspect of the create-maintain-destroy cycle that has been referred to implicitly but not yet explicitly discussed. That is the question of who does the creating, maintaining and destroying. If our hypothetical student who was unable to concentrate were to stay with the awareness continuum, allowing each experience just to be there without resistance or judgments, he would eventually discover that he is the source of his experience.

The self that creates our experience is not the self that we are usually aware of. Most of the time, our attention is taken up with the antics of one of two false selves.

One of these is the Coping Self. This is the part of us that knows how to look good, or, at least, "together." It is the part that puts on an act, that seeks to impress people, that accepts life goals that will get approval and general agreement. It is virtuous, industrious, always in the right.

The other is the Suppressed Self. It's the one that we know all about but try to keep out of the way, and we pretend it doesn't exist. This self is frightened, stingy, unhappy, resentful, distrustful, lazy, doesn't like people, etc., etc.

These two are similar to the Topdog and Underdog of Gestalt therapy, who are in constant battle with one another. Fritz Perls calls them the two clowns. I don't know that it is possible to relate them to specific factors in the chart, since they are both manifestations of the whole chart. There may, however, be some relationship between Topdog and Ascendant plus Midheaven and between Underdog and I.C. plus Descendant. As long as we are involved in the struggle of the two clowns we do not get to be aware of our Real Self, and we run our lives as though we are the victims of our lives.

Behind the Coping Self and the Suppressed Self is the Real Self. It can't be described but only experienced. It can be glimpsed sometimes in meditation, but the problem is that such glimpses seem to come and go and it is often difficult to relate them to living in the world. There are many people who have had blissful peak experiences yet whose lives are in a mess; frequently, they seem less able to cope than those who have not had such experiences.

The Real Self is the space in which our lives happen; it is the source of our lives, our experience, and it includes all that is. To be aligned with the Real Self and have it manifest in the world, we therefore have to be willing to include all that is. And there is an awful lot of stuff that we are not willing to include. Specifically, there are layers of feelings such as pain, anger, anxiety, betrayal, helplessness, aloneness and abandonment. In various ways, we are unwilling to grant existence and validity to such feelings. A lot of the time, we contrive to stay unconscious of them. When they do erupt into consciousness, we hardly ever just let them be and treat them as part of the natural create-maintain-destroy process. We explain them, or justify them or distract ourselves from them. They are so painful and unpleasant that we never suspect that there may be something wonderful on the other side of them. Again, the philosopher's stone doesn't look the way we think it should so we throw it away.

A lot of therapy is concerned with the attempt to break through the layer of negative feelings. This is possible, but very difficult and certainly not the sort of thing one can do all day long. The Gestalt therapists call the layer of suppressed negative feelings the *implosive layer* and describe how a person can be guided through it and into the explosive experience of the authentic self. It works, but it needs the presence of the therapist to push one through all the avoidance and resistance and, unless the explosive experiences are integrated into a coherent world view, they tend to remain isolated and of little more use in the practical world than the blissful peak experiences of the mystic.

So, the Real Self is the source of our lives, of our power and creativity, but the methods generally used to allow it to manifest in the world require special techniques and circumstances. When they work— and they don't seem to work for everybody—the results are spasmodic and difficult to bring together into a coherent life style. What is generally lacking in these methods—therapy and meditation— is a consistent grasp of the truth that we create our lives, that we are each the center of our universe, and that *everything* that is in our lives is there because at some level we intended it to be there.

To have the create-maintain-destroy cycle work for us, so that the issues we are stuck in can clear up, we need to be willing to assume, as a basic working principle, that we are responsible for creating everything that is in our lives.

That does not mean to have a realization of your responsibility, or to have faith in it or to take a position about it. It means choosing to conduct your life as though it were so, no matter what is going on. It is very simple and very difficult, and the mind will pull all manner of tricks to prevent you doing it. A major consequence of assuming responsibility for your life is that you don't get to blame anybody anymore. Not your parents or the government or the economic situation. Not even yourself.

It is a matter of remaining conscious all the time, and it is similar to becoming conscious in a dream. Usually, in so-called lucid dreams, where the dreamer is conscious that he or she is dreaming, the act of becoming conscious alone is enough to clear up negative circumstances in the dream and to create more pleasant conditions. The create-maintain-destroy cycle can work much more quickly at that level. As a practical tip for making your responsibility for your life real for you, consider your life as though it were a dream that you are trying to wake up in. Not wake up *from* but wake up *in*.

Remember that, as we shall see in more detail later, the mind's job is to prevent you doing this. It sees its job as convincing you of the reality of the space-time world and its attendant circumstances. Understanding is a function of the mind, so if you think you *understand* responsibility and create-maintain-destroy, that is not it. Understanding is a particularly subtle trap because it turns the truth of responsibility into a belief system that has no more power than any other. Beliefs, positions and convictions are things, structures which define themselves by being opposed to, or different from, other things and structures. The power does not lie in things but in the context or field within which the things exist. It is not a matter of understanding the idea of responsibility but of "getting" it as you would "get" a joke or a poetic image. The feeling that goes with getting it is amazement, astonishment and a sense of being unlimited.

The statement that you are responsible for creating your life is more like a Zen koan than a piece of information. It is in the same category as the famous, "What is the sound of one hand clapping?" It makes no sense, *in the mind's terms,* and is not intended to make sense.

There are good precedents for assuming that something will work even though it makes no sense in terms of the current accepted paradigm. In mathematics, for example, the idea of the square root of minus one makes no sense at all in the context of ordinary numerical thinking. You can't even begin to get a grip on it. Yet it is a powerful and practical tool. Alternating-current theory makes extensive use of it. If you're reading this by electric light, you are benefiting directly from somebody's use of the square root of minus one. The idea of creating our lives is no more weird than that, and it is more useful to regard it as a powerful and practical tool than as a statement about the nature of reality.

One advantage of being willing to be responsible for creating our lives is that the implosive layer of negative feelings is included as a natural part of the process. In meditation these feelings are bypassed, and in therapy they have to be struggled with. Taking responsibility for negative feelings makes them part of what is. It gradually removes the significance and the judgments that we attach to them.

Being willing to be responsible for creating our lives and being aware of the create-maintain-destroy cycle are all we need, essentially, in order to create a context in which the diagnostic power of the astrological chart can be used effectively. Knowing that we are responsible for our lives, however, is not a function of the reasoning mind. There is no way I can convince you of it intellectually. It's a paradox and all you can do with a paradox is just have it be there. Yet, at another level, it is so obvious. The only reality you have is your experience and, obviously, you are the location, the field, the context in which your experience occurs. You may argue that that still doesn't make you the creator of it. Maybe the planets are creating it and beaming it at you. Maybe your parents did it to you. Maybe there is a personal God devising tests for you. Or—a great favourite in some New Age circles—maybe the Universe has some plan for you that you don't know about yet. Maybe all these things are true, yet they still exist within your experience. There is nothing in your universe but you and your experience, so you get to be responsible for creating the planets and your parents and the personal God and the Universe.

Most people have an experience, usually in childhood or early adolescence, when they suddenly realize that they are unique, that they are, in fact, at the center of the entire universe. The feeling that usually accompanies the experience is one of astonishment. It is also accompanied by the realization that it is impossible to see the universe from any other point of view, that one is always trapped in one's own head.

I suggest you search your memory for any such experience that may have occurred to you because it is that quality of direct experience that we are interested in, not concepts of it. Of course, the memory will be a memory and not the experience but at least you will know that you have had first hand knowledge of what we are talking about.

However, this experience of being the center of the universe does not seem to have any practical consequences and we generally dismiss the whole thing. Again, it's the philosopher's stone; the experience that can transform our lives is there all the time, it can be had for the asking, and it looks as though it had no practical value whatever, so we throw it away.

Although the only way to find out whether creating your reality is true or not is to experience it, it's interesting to look at it in the light of modern physics.

Classical physics postulated a universe of things, operating according to clearly defined mechanical laws, objectively "out there" acting and reacting in a sequence of cause and effect independently of human observers. This model, of course, is still believed in—in an unconscious, unexamined way—by most people, including a lot of astrologers who still imagine that a purely mechanical, cause and effect explanation of astrology will one day be forthcoming. There is good reason to go on believing in it because it accurately accounts for just about everything we meet with in our everyday experience.

In fact, it is an approximation to the truth. It works very well as long as we are only concerned with handling and manipulating the physical environment. At least, it works very well on its own terms. Some of its byproducts, like the hydrogen bomb and environmental pollution, can hardly be cited as evidence of it working well in terms of enhancing the quality of people's lives.

In the old, classical physics, it used to be thought that the ultimate building bricks of matter were atoms, which were thought of as hard separate entities like miniature billiard balls. It was assumed that the known laws of mechanics could be applied to them, and that the properties of matter could be fully understood by assuming that atoms and molecules did, in fact, behave in all respects like minute billiard balls. For a long time, up to the end of the nineteenth century, this approach worked. The actual behaviour of matter at ordinary levels does correspond very closely indeed with the mathematical formulae derived from the "billiard ball" theory.

Just before the turn of the century, X rays and the electron were discovered, showing that the atom has a fine structure and could no longer be treated as a solid ball. Moreover, it was soon discovered that the subatomic particles were infinitesimally small in comparison with the atom itself, tiny though that was. A model of the atom that was used for a time was that it consisted of an arrangement like a minute solar system, with negative electrons orbiting a central nucleus made up of positive protons and neutral neutrons. To get some idea of the scale of atomic structure we have to suppose that an individual atom is enlarged to the size of a cathedral dome. On that scale, the nucleus, at the center, would be about the size of a grain of salt, and the electrons, orbiting the edge of the dome, would be hardly visible specks of dust.

None of this is exactly new stuff; I imagine many readers have come across it before, but it generally remains stuck at the level of information. Like the experience of being the center of our universe, it doesn't seem to have any practical consequences in our lives, unless we are scientists or engineers, and even then it doesn't have practical consequences outside the laboratory. However, we can create it having practical consequences just by staying aware that the seemingly solid objects out in the universe are in fact a lot less substantial than they look.

Contemplating the picture of the structure of the atom, and that it in fact consists mostly of nothing, must, at the least, invite us to question the assumptions that we make so automatically and unconsciously about physical reality. But this is not the end of the matter. Physicists at first assumed that the electrons and protons could be treated as though they, in turn, were infinitesimal billiard balls. However, it soon became apparent that they behaved as much like waves as like particles, and it was disconcerting to find that an electron, which did in some ways behave like a solid particle, could be in two places at once. And, to boggle the mind a little more, if the ultimate constituents of matter are waves, what are they waves in? Nothing, obviously. It becomes impossible for the mind to make any kind of model or picture of ultimate physical reality. Evidently we construct our universe according to what the mind *can* grasp.

At the ultimate level of physical matter, matter itself turns out to be completely mutable. All particles—there are now known to be some 200 varieties—can be transmuted into each other, can be created from pure energy, and can be destroyed, or transformed back into energy. The whole universe appears as a web of energy patterns, each interlinked with the other. There is no such thing as an isolated, separate object. All there is is a continuous process of create-maintain-destroy, operating as an inseparable whole which always includes the observer. The familiar world of separate things, of space and time, is an illusion, a construct that we agree upon. It is as though we all, as our Real Selves, have agreed on a set of rather limiting rules to do with space, time, energy and matter in order that we can play certain games.

I find it useful to think of the Real Self as being like an actor who puts himself into the part he is playing so wholeheartedly that he becomes identified with the part he is playing and forgets who he really is. We will be looking in detail at the issue of creating the kind of negativities that we do create in the next chapter, but this analogy already gives us a hint. Any actor who is capable of the part would be delighted at the opportunity of playing Hamlet. He would regard it as an exciting challenge to his skill and a wonderful opportunity for self-expression. But nobody would want to *be* Hamlet, at Hamlet's level of consciousness. Your father is murdered, your mother commits incest, your girlfriend drowns herself and you wind up being stabbed to death by a poisoned sword—who needs it? An actor who really believed that he was Hamlet would feel completely the victim of all these circumstances, yet the truth is that he chose them—and for no more reason than that he wanted to. It seemed like a good idea at the time.

The equivalent of getting the part of Hamlet is that the Real Self—that is, you and me—creates a vehicle, the body-mind, which has one purpose and one purpose only, and that is to survive in the physical, space-time world. Not only to survive physically but to ensure the survival of the beliefs and feelings, thoughts and attitudes that the mind thinks are an essential part of it. Hamlet has a very powerful belief system about the necessity of avenging his honor—however dilatory and indecisive he may be about carrying that out. In the end, he would rather have his body die than give up, or even examine the validity of, that belief. In fact, this is the tragedy of Hamlet. For all his endless introspection it never once occurs to him to suppose that his drive for revenge is anything other than some kind of ultimate truth. The survival drive of the body-mind—which we will refer to simply as the mind from now on—is so powerful that the Real Self is trapped in it and thinks that it *is* the mind and that there is nothing else.

It is hardly possible to overestimate the power, subtlety and tenacity of the mind's drive for survival. This is why it is so difficult to get hold of and see the value in the notions and principles that we are exploring here. "Sure, it's interesting to suppose I create my life. I even agree with it in a way, especially if physics says that must be the way things are, but it's no practical use to me when I've got a bill to pay and no money in the bank." That's the mind talking.

The yogis in India have a very good analogy for the way the mind works. It seems that a method of catching monkeys in India was to take a gourd, hollow it out, put some nuts in it and leave a hole in the side big enough for the monkey's outstretched hand to go in but not big enough for his clenched fist, with the nuts in it, to come out. Along comes the hungry monkey, totally concerned with survival; no other thought enters his head. He puts his hand in the gourd, grabs the nuts, and then, of course, is stuck. He rages and thrashes about and struggles like crazy but the one thing he won't do is let go of the nuts. He doesn't even know that it might be an option. Like Hamlet, he would rather die than give up his belief that those particular nuts are necessary for his survival. This is how the mind works. The yogis further say that, if we imagine that the monkey is drunk and is being constantly stung by angry bees, this is even more like the way the mind works.

This is what we are up against and what, as astrologers, our clients are up against. In some ways, a human being is in a worse position than the monkey. He usually doesn't even know that he is holding onto the nuts. A major service that the astrologer can perform is to get him clear about that and about what kind of nuts he is holding on to. No wonder it's difficult. No wonder it's so hard to "let the psychic processes grow in peace." Very difficult thing to do when you're trapped, starving to death, crazy with booze and being stung by angry bees!

In yoga, this story is usually told as a preliminary to explaining the virtues of meditation as a technique for stilling the mind, which amounts to giving the monkey a powerful sedative. This may work, for some people, but, in the end, it is just another way of resisting what is. As I remarked earlier, all that pain and struggle is bypassed rather than included. If being our Real Selves means including all that is, then the only way to do it is by having compassion for the mind—the poor, trapped, struggling monkey. It also means being constantly aware of what the monkey is up to. A statement that is frequently attributed to Thomas Jefferson is, "The price of liberty is eternal vigilance." That was said in a political context, but it is just as true of liberating ourselves from the tyranny of our minds.

The point is that the monkey originally *chose* to put his hand in the gourd, and all his subsequent troubles come from resisting the consequences of his choice and believing himself to be the victim of these consequences. All he really has to do is let go of the nuts and go and look for a supply that isn't booby-trapped, but his survival drive will not let him do that.

One can say that the whole issue of having our lives work depends on rehabilitating, reclaiming, our original power of choice and discovering what the truth is about it, what we can choose and what we can't.

There is a story from Plato's *Republic* that I find very useful for illustrating this point, and I frequently tell it to clients as part of the preliminary discussion. It is not entirely logically consistent with the other analogies I have used but, in the realm we have entered, poetic truth is a better guide than logical consistency.

In the story, a man named Er is seemingly killed in battle, and he goes with many others to a place where souls are about to cast lots for the privilege of choosing the lives that they will live on earth in the next incarnation. One of the Fates, Lachesis, has lots and patterns of lives on her lap. An interpreter addresses the assembled souls and tells them that the one who draws the first lot shall be the first to choose a life which then will be his by necessity. He tells them that the responsibility for the choice is not God's but that of the soul who makes the choice.

Er is forbidden to choose; he is told that he is there simply as a messenger to report the proceedings back to the world of men. The interpreter sets many different patterns of life on the ground, far more than there are souls to choose from them, and of every conceivable kind. For the most part, the souls choose their lives unconsciously, impelled by unfinished business from previous lives. The man who has the first choice chooses the life of a great king. In his haste and greed, he fails to read the small print and does not realize at first that part of his fate is to kill his wife and eat his children and have all kinds of horrors. This soul had been a good man in his previous life, but out of habit and custom rather than a genuine perception of the truth. When he realizes the full consequences of his choice, it is too late to change. He curses the gods and blames everybody but himself for his unfortunate fate.

The soul of Orpheus chooses to be born as a swan. Orpheus had been killed by being torn to pieces by women, and he is unwilling to be born of a woman after such a death at their hands. Odysseus, who had lived a life of adventurous suffering, looks around for a long time until he finds a totally ordinary and uneventful life and then chooses it with joy. (The story doesn't record whether he went crazy with the boredom of it later, but doubtless he did!) Generally, the rest of the souls choose as a result of past habits, either to continue them or in reaction against them, as did Orpheus and Odysseus. When all the souls have chosen they drink the waters of Lethe, which cause them to forget everything that has happened, and they are born into the lives they have chosen.

The story needs little comment. I have no privileged information on whether something like that actually does take place before we are born. That is not the point. The point is that the story can assist us to be willing to assume that we create our reality and to be responsible for it.

After telling my client the story from Plato, I then usually make it more personal by saying maybe the way it is between lives is something like this: It's like you're an out-of-work actor, and you're getting so bored and fed up with being out of work that you'll do *anything* to get back onto the stage and have your name in lights again. One day you're sitting around there, bored out of your mind, convinced that you'll never work again and, suddenly, God comes out of the office with a script under his arm, comes over to you and says, "Boy, have I got a winner for you this time!" You don't even ask what the salary is you're so keen to get back into the space-time drama. Your birth chart is a coded version of that script that God came out of the office with. What we're going to do in this session is decode the chart so you get a chance to remember and get conscious again about the script, the drama that you're starring in, and you get a chance to remember who you really are.

This usually sets the tone of the session effectively. Many people find it at least mildly amusing and usually lighten up; and a space is created that facilitates them looking at the basic issues of their lives.

Though the choice of a particular script is made outside the space-time world, we recapitulate the essence of it in various ways in early life. It is easier for the mind to grasp the idea of the formation of the script in childhood, and it is useful to have some understanding of the process of the way we react to parental influences. As I remarked earlier, there is no power, of itself, in understanding the past, but it frequently aids clarity in the present and clarity is an essential first step. In the next chapter, we shall look at the process of script formation in the early years of childhood.

3

Life Patterns: The Script

Rather than consider that childhood difficulties lay the foundations for problems in later life, from the point of view of taking responsibility for them it is more workable to think of the things that happened in childhood as being trial runs of the drama. Having chosen our role, outside of space and time, once we get into the space-time world we proceed to act it out with whatever vehicle and circumstances are available to us. The nine months from conception may be a kind of rehearsal period, but from the moment of birth, when the natal chart comes into effect, the curtain is up and the show is on.

There seems to be a good deal of evidence for the reality of the so-called "birth trauma." The actual process of birth is thought to establish deep automatic patterns that govern the rest of our lives. For example, if the baby almost suffocates for lack of air, a general fearful expectation of *scarcity* will be established which will manifest later perhaps as the inability to get love or enough money. Or, if the baby is immediately taken away from the mother and placed in a hospital crib, there will be a pattern established of going through life expecting little human warmth and contact. Some types of therapy aim, by various means, to have the client relive the experiences of birth on the assumption that doing so will remove the compulsive patterns of later life. People do indeed experience feelings and sensations that seem to relate to the birth process, and these feelings are a reflection of their major life problems. It is much more dramatic than the intellectual insights of conventional psychoanalysis, and it frequently gives the client access to emotions that had been blocked. In broader terms, however, all that usually happens is that the client shifts the blame from his parents to the birth trauma and still doesn't gain access to his own power and intention in the matter.

I don't think we need quarrel with the idea that the birth trauma exists and that patterns are set so early. I have sometimes done charts for very small children at the request of parents. I have been surprised by the feedback from the parents who say that their children of just a few weeks old are manifesting, however crudely, the characteristics shown in the charts. This, of course, is long before the patterns of parental influence can be supposed to have taken effect.

The question is not whether the birth trauma exists but whether it is useful to us for our present purpose of developing a framework for the effective use of astrology. Since the material relating to the birth trauma is only accessible in special circumstances, and not always then (not everybody can be successfully hypnotized or regressed), it is not really of much immediate use. Much more accessible is the layer of parental influence, and some understanding of the dynamics of that is very useful to the astrological counselor. That is, always providing that he or she doesn't get stuck in believing it to be the *source* of the problem. It seems necessary to repeat this caveat since the weight of conventional psychological opinion is that it *is* the source of the problem. And this is most certainly the popular view of conventional psychological opinion.

It is possible to work effectively just using the chart and the model of prelife choice and responsibility that we have discussed. Indeed, it is fairly rare for me to spend much time on parental influence during an actual session with a client, though at one time I paid a great deal of attention to it. Sometimes, however, the space that the client is in makes it necessary. One just has to be able to handle the matter in order to move on. Also, the parental influence stage of the drama is pretty nearly as stark and simple as the birth trauma and, with the method I shall present in this chapter, comparatively easy to understand and, if necessary, to elucidate and to present to the cient.

The technique I am going to describe is that of Transactional Analysis—TA for short. It seems to me the simplest and most coherent way of looking at how emotional patterns are formed—or rather how the prelife choice manifests during the drama of parental influence. It is almost impossible to avoid using reactive language in describing the process, and I will follow the usual convention of talking as though the child is a separate and vulnerable entity completely molded by the emotional pressures of the environment. Indeed, to the mind, that is exactly the way it is. The problem is analogous to that of physics: in order to talk about events in the ordinary world, we have to use ordinary language.

What follows is not to be taken as a belief system or even necessarily as an accurate model of the way things are. As we have seen, ultimately there aren't any models. However, it is a lucid and convenient way of describing some of the processes that go on in the mind. The real purpose of it is to facilitate, to open a space for, the actual experience of what is. When you are experiencing the truth, it doesn't matter what scaffolding you have used to assist yourself to arrive at the experience. Once you have arrived at a destination it is of no importance whatever whether the train was labeled Freud, Jung, TA, Gestalt or even astrology itself.

Transactional Analysis was begun by Eric Berne, a Californian psychiatrist, in the late 1950s. It is essentially a Freudian-oriented, reactive concept, and it is now very much more elaborate than the basic model of it than I shall give here. The particular value of it, for our purposes, is its concept of the "script" or "life-script." The TA idea of the script is that it is a life plan which contains all the significant things that a person will do and be and have happen to him. It is not something decided by fate, or the gods, but has its origins in premature *decisions* about life made in childhood.

Apart from the disagreement about the point of origin of the script (which is to be expected), the definition amounts to the same as the one we are working with. TA puts a lot of emphasis on the importance of the script being the result of a decision on the part of the small person. It doesn't, however, really see him as having much choice. Since he is quite literally dependent on his parents, as a matter of life and death, the choice according to TA, is either to go along with the way things are around here or to die. As the level at which the intention operates is not properly recognized, the ultimate effectiveness of Transactional Analysis is rather limited, but its value at the level of information is very high.

In order to understand script formation, we first have to understand the way Transactional Analysis sees the structure of the mind. It starts from the observation that we all operate from three "ego-states," the Parent, the Adult and the Child. Capital letters distinguish these words as technical terms from the same words used in the ordinary sense. This simple original structure has been the subject of considerable discussion and elaboration since it was first propounded, but it remains effective and will serve perfectly well for our purposes.

The Parent is derived from the way actual parents and other authority figures behaved when you were small. When in this ego state,

*Claude M. Steiner, *SCRIPTS PEOPLE LIVE,* NEW YORK:Grove Press Inc., 1974, p. 53.

you talk, act and respond to others in the way in which some parental figure did. Even when you are not exhibiting the Parent state it acts internally as a source both of inhibitions and of permissions to do things. The Parent functions as a storehouse of ways of disciplining and ways of nurturing. It can therefore conveniently be divided into Critical Parent (CP) and Nurturing Parent (NP).

The Adult is a state of logical, objective functioning. When you are in your Adult you consider and appraise situations coolly on the basis of past experience. The Adult deals with facts and the deductions to be made from those facts. It is your own Mr. Spock, immune to emotion. There is some tendency in TA literature to suggest that the Adult is the most valuable of the three states. It is not, but it *is* the essential one in taking the first step to clearing up patterns—that is, becoming clearly conscious of them.

The Child ego state is pretty much what it says. It is that part of us that has remained a little boy or girl of, usually, between two and five years of age. It contains our power, drives, instincts, our capacity for love, hate, creativity, sexuality, intuition, joy, ecstasy. It is not to be regarded as "childish" or "immature"; these are Parent judgment words. Eric Berne says that the Child is the most valuable part of the personality. It is the most archaic part, in touch with mystery, magic and poetry. It is the Child in us who knows the truth about being the creator of our universe.

Again, it is convenient to divide the Child into two parts, the Natural Child (NC) and Adapted Child (AC). The qualities described in the last paragraph belong to the Natural Child. The Adapted Child is the part that has learned patterns of behavior in order to be accepted and to survive. The ego states are shown in Fig. 1.3.1.

Figure 1.3.1 Ego States. P = Parent; A = Adult; C = Child.

In this way, we can use the following figures to clarify the interactions that take place between people.

a)
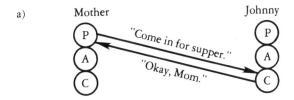

b)
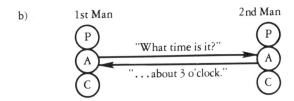

c)

Figure 1.3.2 a) Parent to Child: One person in authority relationship to another. b) Adult to Adult: Unemotional seeking of information. c) Child to Child: Fun-loving child appeals to fun-loving child of the other.

The other person need not reply from the same ego state that is being addressed. In Fig. 1.3.2c the woman may indeed say "I'd love to" from her Child. She could also reply "Not if you were the last man on earth" (Parent) or "I have to work tonight" (Adult). The time-honoured excuse of "I have to stay in and wash my hair" would be Adapted Child. ("I don't want to go out with you but I can't say so directly.")

Messages that activate the Child state are always apt to be powerful. In some circumstances, they can seem like irresistible demands. This is especially so when they come from the powerful Child state of the actual mother or father and activate the highly responsive Child state of the little boy or girl. These, in fact, are the foundations of the script. They are not usually overtly stated but conveyed nonverbally. They can almost always be expressed as injunctions not to do or be something.

For example, the parents may have been extremely set on having a boy and they get a girl. They swallow their disappointment and go on hoping for a boy next time. Overtly, their behavior to their daughter may be kind and nurturing but there will be a message going from the sulky disappointed Child state in both mother and father to the Child state of the daughter that says "Don't be a girl." This is not a script but it is the foundation of a script and is shown in figure 1.3.3.

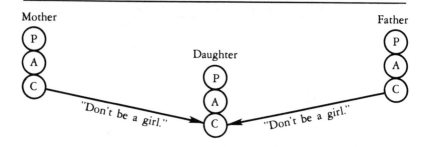

Figure 1.3.3 Child-state of parents to Child-state of daughter

The Child to Child messages, delivered in these circumstances, are known as injunctions. They have the binding force of legal injunctions—greater actually, since it is at least possible to act against a legal injunction even if the consequences are unpleasant, but it isn't even possible to act against script injunctions once they have been accepted. Not at the level at which they are implanted, that is; obviously one acts against them at other, less powerful, levels.

It must be remembered that the Child of the little girl experiences her mother and father as omnipotent beings and she is, absolutely literally, dependent on them for her survival. She makes the decision that the way to survive in the world is not to be a girl. In the monkey analogy, this is equivalent to the monkey grabbing a nut labeled, "I won't be a girl" and refusing to give it up because her survival depends on it. Clearly, a major issue for this person is going to be her own femininity and her ability to fully relate to the world as a woman. Notice that there may not be any particularly traumatic or painful incidents for her to recall in later life. The script will have been set by the all-pervasive sense that being female is somehow not quite acceptable.

Another way of getting a sense of how powerful these script injunctions are is to consider that human beings have an intense hunger for structure. Without some sense of support and structure there is great fear and panic. To get some idea of what it is like for a small child, suppose you woke up one morning and found you had been mysteriously transported during the night to the streets of a foreign city, in a not too salubrious area, where you didn't speak a word of the language. In these circumstances, structure hunger would be overwhelming. You would be very likely to grab hold of, and act on, the first coherent direction you could get, regardless of how ill-advised it might turn out to be later on.

In the same way, we might suppose that the first coherent direction for our little girl, trying to figure out how to make it in her baffling and frightening new world, is the sense of "Don't be a girl." She fastens onto it eagerly because it is at least structure, something she can rely on. She makes a *decision* about it and commits creative intention to not being a girl, and this then becomes a reality-creating pattern. Given the circumstances in which she makes it, it is a right decision and a smart decision. The trouble is, she will spend the rest of her life justifying it and proving herself right about it, long after it has ceased to be appropriate.

A script structure is more complicated than this and, for a more detailed look at one, consider the following scenario. This time we have a small boy. His mother is bright, kind and intelligent but has considerable difficulties with her own sexuality and the giving of physical love. Father is reliable, conscientious, a professional man who works hard but never quite gets the success he feels he deserves and is somewhat embittered. He is courteous and rather reserved.

Generally, the most powerful script injunction comes from the parent of the opposite sex. As the little boy (let's call him John) starts out in the world he immediately gets the message from his mother that there is something unpleasant for her in cuddling him and breast-feeding him, and that there is something unpleasant about his own needs for intensely loving physical contact.

The injunction here is "Don't be close." Out of his overwhelming structure hunger, John seizes on the "Don't be close" injunction as his way of surviving, of making it through life. He has already decided that this is how his life is going to be. In the early months of life it isn't too complicated to carry this decision out. All he has to do is tense up and withdraw a little whenever he is held and fed. No great problems so far.

Later, when he learns to walk and talk and his awareness of the environment is expanded, he discovers that he needs more information on how not to be close to people. So he looks to his father as a role model. He sees father being reserved, courteous, helpful to others in a detached way. At this stage, he will also start to pick up the injunction from his father's Child, "Don't make it."

Overtly, his mother from her Parent may be giving him prescriptions for living such as "Always be considerate." His father, from his Parent, may be saying things like "If you want to get anywhere in this world, you have to work hard." These messages go from Parent to Parent and they become the "Counter-script"—what John consciously believes as opposed to what he has unconsciously already decided (see figure 1.3.4). By the time he about five years old he has fully decided how his life is going to be.

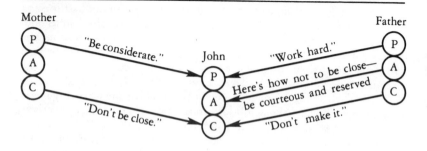

Figure 1.3.4 The script and counter-script.

To get an idea of one way in which the script might work out as John grows up, let's suppose that, apart from the problem with physical love, his mother is excellent. She makes sure he is well fed and clothed, she is conscientious about his education and takes a knowledgeable interest in his interests. He has no reason to think that there is anything missing. The fact that his parents never show much affection for each other or for him is just the way the world is.

Somehow, emotional intimacy is never an issue. He feels uneasy when he is watching TV with his parents around and there is a love scene or an emotional parent-child relationship. Or, when other people behave demonstratively with him or with each other, he tenses up a little and holds back. It doesn't really bother him but it seems faintly wrong. He would rather not have anything to do with it. He will probably not experience the truly damaging limitations of his script decision until such time as he is strongly sexually attracted to a woman.

Remember that, at the unconscious reality-creating level, his very survival depends on not making it and not being close. Paradoxically, at this level, emotional fulfillment is actually seen as a threat that can open up the chaotic, unstructured panic. That part of his mind that is imprinted with the script thinks that, at all costs, to protect him and ensure his survival, it *must* prevent him from making it and getting close to people. It cannot stop him falling in love—at least we are assuming it doesn't since we are assuming a "normal neurotic" development, not a severe pathology—but it will ensure that he only falls in love with women who will reject him or who are in other ways unsuitable. He will take very good care that he doesn't fall in love with a woman who loves him and with whom there are no obstacles to a close relationship.

As John grows up, he knows consciously that the way for him to be in the world is to work hard and to be considerate of others. He is conscientious and reliable. He generally acts with a lot of integrity, and people tend to feel good around him because he can be trusted and is considerate of their needs and feelings. Almost always friendly and courteous, he gives the impression of something held in reserve even though he is sociable. People, especially women, find this reserve attractive. His relationships with women invariably leave the woman feeling unsatisfied and rejected on a subtle level even though John pays her every attention and gives her every consideration. (The women, of course, have some kind of complementary scripts that call for them to have disappointing experiences with men. There are no innocent bystanders!)

John's inner experience is bewildered despair. He does all the things he is supposed to do and yet he doesn't make it with women in any really satisfying way. Soon, he starts to notice that he isn't making it in any other way either. He doesn't do as well in examinations as he expected and as everyone expected of him. Eventually he settles down into a job that is well below his potential and resigns himself to being a bachelor.

After a while he becomes gently cynical and embittered and convinces himself that this is the way he prefers it. All the time he is being run by his script, pretty nearly as rigidly as the script of a play. Unconsciously he seeks out people and situations that fit in with the demands of his script.

This may sound rigidly deterministic and, at the level we are talking about, it is. John has no control over his script. He is absolutely fated to have frustrated relationships with women and to fail to live up to his potential. That is, as long as he is unwilling to take responsibility for being the source of his script. As long as he thinks that, somehow, "life" has done this to him he is stuck in the script. This will remain true even though he goes to a therapist and gets considerable insight into the problem. The amount of creative will available to John as a thirty-year-old man is nothing compared to the creative will available to John as a panic-stricken baby, desperately grasping at some way of surviving in an alien world.

The forces at work in the creation of the script may be compared with nuclear energy. The forces available to the conscious ego may, correspondingly, be compared to the energies of an ordinary chemical reaction. It gives a sense of the issue to say that attempting to destroy a script by conscious determination to go against it is rather like trying to stop a chain reaction in uranium by pouring acid on it. A chemical reaction may take place but it is not relevant to the essential issue.

These concepts make the process of parental influence easy to understand and to present to a client. Moreover, if it should be desirable, a working approximation of the client's script can fairly easily be deduced. This can be very useful with the type of client who has had little experience of looking at his or her own motivations. Basically, all that is necessary is to ask the client to describe his parents and then look at the way the parents were in terms of messages of ways to be.

One way of doing this is to have a set of prepared questions that will get to the root of the matter. They can be given to the client ahead of time and you can ask him or her to mail the answers to you before the session. The questions are:

1. Describe your father briefly.
2. Describe your mother briefly.
3. What was your father's advice to you about life? If no direct advice, what nonverbal message did you pick up by observing the way he conducted himself in the world?
4. Answer the same question for your mother.
5. If you wrote a play about your father's life, what would the title be?
6. What would the title be for a play about your mother's life?
7. What did your father least want you to do?
8. What did your mother least want you to do?

A typical set of answers is given from a client who was severely underachieving because of a powerful sense of inferiority, though he behaved in a confident, breezy, even aggressive manner. He was an outstanding amateur actor and wanted to become a professional, but his sense of inferiority had never allowed him to make the move. The answers to the questions were:

1. A warm man but not able to communicate. Loved children, especially girls—not really at home with small boys. Very confident with his own

sort. In his youth, very forceful and very much his own man. The sadness of his marriage and continued poverty affected him greatly. Very protective of his children and had great respect for his wife. Religious and humble.

2. A proud woman. Leaned very much towards her daughters, who were always able to confide in her. (The client was the only son and youngest child of a family of four.) She never really loved my father but looked to him for comfort and security. She had a kind of affection for me but regarded me as useless at anything she considered important.

3. Get away from home. (Londonderry, Northern Ireland, where opportunitites were very poor.)

4. You need a good woman to make something of you.

5. The Humble Ploughboy.

6. Mother of Sorrows.

7. No clear answer.

8. Get married. Become an actor.

It is easy to see from these answers that there was a severe devaluing of masculinity yet an emphasis on being proud and independent at another level. It is a fair guess that the injunctions from both parents were "Don't be a man." Father provides the "here's how" by being humble and embittered. The Parent advice is not altogether clear but it is something like "Get away from home and be independent," which is certainly what the client was attempting to do. He had been living in England, out of contact with his family, for some years and at one time had been a merchant seaman. A tentative script matrix for this man is shown in figure 1.3.5.

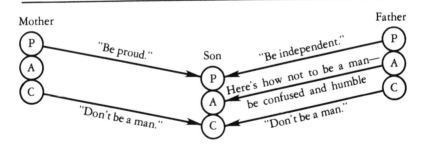

Figure 1.3.5 A proud underachiever.

Of course, it must not be supposed that such a relatively simple procedure gives us a fully validated script but, for our purposes, that is not necessary. It does provide a starting point and a tool for assisting the client to develop some clarity as to what is actually going on in his life.

I want to emphasize that I see the use of TA concepts as being an adjunct to the use of the astrological chart, much as event astrologers will sometimes use tarot to obtain extra information. It is by no means central to the approach being developed in this book, but with some clients it can be extremely helpful.

In my experience, it is not particularly useful to attempt to find exact relationships between the script diagram and the chart. It is certainly possible. The Moon and Saturn often seem to be connected with the injunctions and the Midheaven seems to reflect the counter-script. Some attributes of Mercury obviously fit with the definition of the Adult. However, the astrological symbolism is much the richer of the two systems, and to attempt to relate it specifically to the TA script is to limit it. With enough research and experience it might be possible to draw the script matrix directly from the chart, without using the questionnaire, but such research and experience are not available.

For readers who want to find out more about Transactional Analysis, there are many books available. I particularly recommend *Scripts People Live* by Claude M. Steiner, Grove Press Inc., New York, 1974.

4

The Hidden Power

We are now in a position to start to look at where the actual power that controls our lives is so we can do something about it. The difficulty is that there is total incompatibility between experiencing the power and talking about it. As the Zen saying has it, "Those who know don't tell and those who tell don't know." Knowing is essentially a wordless, nonrational experience. When I am engaged in knowing, I cannot, by definition, be telling. When I am engaged in telling, I cannot, by definition be knowing. To do the two things together is as impossible as going north and south at the same time.

To get a practical sense of the issue, consider the following piece of poetry. When you are reading it, as far as possible suspend judgments. Don't compare it with other poetry. Never mind whether you like it or not. Just allow yourself to be with it and allow the poetry to work on you. Allow yourself to *experience* the poetry.

> The barge she sat in, like a burnish'd throne
> Burn'd on the water. The poop was beaten gold;
> Purple the sails, and so perfumed that
> The winds were love-sick with them; the oars were silver,
> Which to the tune of flutes kept stroke, and made
> The water which they beat to follow faster,
> As amorous of their strokes......
>
> ....The city cast
> Her people out upon her; and Antony,
> Enthron'd i' th' market-place, did sit alone,

Whistling to th' air; which, but for vacancy,
Had gone to gaze on Cleopatra too,
And made a gap in nature.*

You might want to read it two or three times to get the full impact of it. Notice and experience the effect. Then notice that, at one level, it could be reduced to a flat statement that Cleopatra came to town in her barge and everybody except Antony rushed out to meet her.

The difference between that flat statement and the experience of the poetry is the difference between having information about something and knowing it. Notice that once you start to talk about the experience you are no longer experiencing it. You can describe the poem, talk about its impact on you, discuss how the poet gets his effects, remark on the things that don't quite come off and so on. This can be a very interesting and enjoyable way of spending time but it has nothing whatever to do with the wordless aliveness of the poetry itself.

The subject matter, the content, of the verse is, as it happens, itself pleasurable and enjoyable but it need not have been. Much poetry that conveys that authentic experience of aliveness has themes that are sad, boring, horrifying or disgusting. It is as if the poet takes the raw material of experience, whatever it may be, and *by accepting it* gets back to the experience of creative aliveness that it came from. So it is with our lives. We can get to that experience just as well from unpleasant feelings as from pleasant ones. A "loser" script like the ones described in the last chapter is just as good a starting point as a "winner" script.

The point is that knowing the themes of one's life intellectually or being highly aware of the feelings one has about them is not at all the same thing as being in touch with the wordless, creative aliveness that they come from. As I have said before, this is where most therapy and certainly most forms of astrological practice get stuck.

It is as though we live in an invisible cage which is made up of the unconscious decisions we have made about our lives. We literally cannot do anything or feel anything or think or say anything outside of that cage. It is as though we are born with tight-fitting red goggles. Not only does everything look red, we cannot experience the redness. We don't even *know* it looks red because red is all there is. We have drunk the waters of Lethe so that we don't even know we are starring in a drama. Except that what we are up to now is getting our memory back.

*William Shakespeare, *Antony and Cleopatra,* London & Glasgow: Collins, 1978, Act 2, Scene 2.

We need a word to refer to the all-pervading redness of the analogy. The trouble with the word "script" is that it largely refers to the *mechanism* that controls our lives, and I want to get back to the energy that powers the mechanism and that the mechanism actually comes from. Or, to come back to the analogy of the poem, I want us to have our attention on the experience of the poetry and not on the words that are the vehicle of the experience.

Werner Erhard, the founder of the *est* training, uses the word "context" to describe the basic way of perceiving life that gives shape and significance to all our experience. It is a good word, showing the importance of the background against which, and within which, a given experience occurs. For example, consider the word "astrology" and see how its meaning shifts when placed in the following contexts: (1) a book, such as this one, which is concerned with the fundamental essence of what astrology is about; (2) a serious book or article on the mechanics of chart interpretation; (3) a "lucky stars" column in a newspaper; (4) a hostile article by a so-called scientist who is convinced it is all rubbish. The word changes its meaning quite radically, and its meanings in the first and fourth examples are almost totally opposed.

Context is not a thing or a mechanism. It is a potential that generates and operates through a mechanism, as the poetry generates and operates through a certain arrangement of words. A context absolutely sets the tone for and determines the outcome of all events that take place within it. You cannot change the context by manipulating the content. We all try to do this yet it is as absurd as trying to change a war movie into a love story by putting a different screen in front of the projector.

Suppose that, on a table top, there are a number of unmagnetized compass needles, pivoted so that they can move freely about their centers. They are all pointing in different directions. Now you switch on a powerful magnetic field. This generates secondary fields in the needles and they all swing round and point north. You can say that the field acts on the needles in a mechanical way and makes them point north. This is true but it misses the actual power of the system at the nonmechanical level. The whole system is totally imbued with the quality of northness. Maybe you decide that, in spite of this, you want one of the needles to point east. You reach out and turn it so that it is pointing east. If you let go of it, it will swing back to point north. If you spend the rest of your life holding it to point east you still have not made the slightest difference to the essential northness of it. You are not creating eastness in the needle, you are merely resisting northness in a way that looks like eastness. It takes a lot of time and attention and is very exhausting.

The context is not the magnetic field itself but the condition of northness which envelops everything within it, including those things that don't look as if they have the quality of northness. It is crucial to get this and I am aware that I am repeating the same material in different ways. I am doing this because the power of context cannot be grasped by the mind.

In the example given in the last chapter, the context of John's life is lovelessness and, for the sake of clarity, I described a possible manifestation of this in such a way that it obviously looked loveless. But we may suppose that John spends a good deal of time "fixing" the needles so that they point east. By sheer force of effort, he may establish relationships with women that have a high emotional charge and a good deal of permanence. He may convince himself, and everyone else, that he is actually good at relating to women. Yet, until he confronts the context of his life and creates a new one, everything he does will be an expression of lovelessness.

Another image that may assist us to "get" context is the image that Jung used for the archetypes—which are themselves contexts. He said that they may be compared with the invisible presence of a crystal lattice in a saturated solution. (For readers who do not remember their elementary chemistry, a saturated solution is made by dissolving as much of a crystal substance—say copper sulphate—as possible in water at a high temperature. As the solution cools, the copper sulphate slowly forms crystals.) The invisible presence of the lattice can hardly be said to exist in any sense in which we normally use the word, any more than "northness" exists in terms of normal usage, yet it absolutely determines the shape of the crystals that manifest.

A real life example of the creation and manifestation of a context— and also of how little it is understood or even recognized—is the development of powered flight. Up to about 1899, when Wilbur Wright began to investigate the problem, the world was operating out of a context that heavier than air flight was impossible. Somehow, the Wright brothers created a context called "powered flight is a reality" and from then on it was inevitable that they should succeed in flying. Once they were operating from the context of the reality of powered flight, then they did the right things and problems that needed to be solved were solved. Other experimenters had exactly the same facts available to them as did the Wright brothers. They were not able to make successful use of them because they were coming from the context of the impossibility of flight. Presumably they *believed* that flight was possible or they would not have spent so much time, energy and money in pursuing it, but the other experimenters were using their beliefs to resist the existing context instead of creating a new one.

To see how little the power of context is appreciated and recognized, it is only necessary to reflect on the image most people have of the Wright brothers. Air travel has made a difference in the lives of just about everyone on the planet, directly or indirectly. Yet most people, if they think about Wilbur and Orville Wright at all, think of them as a pair of clever bicycle mechanics who tinkered about with funny-looking contraptions in their spare time and were lucky enough to stumble on the secret of flight. And it was just chance that they did so before someone else. The truth is that no one else was even close to success when Wilbur made the first flight on December 17, 1903 (at 12.00 hrs EST, Kitty Hawk, North Carolina—a close Sun, Uranus, Midheaven conjunction). Other experimenters were not even on the right track and their findings proved to be almost useless to the Wrights, who not only created the first airplane but also created a workable science of aerodynamics which ensured the development of flying.

This example also illustrates how useless belief is unless it is aligned with the context within which it exists. Just believing that they could fly got the other pioneers nowhere. We are told that thought is creative, that if we want something we should believe in it, visualize it or verbally affirm that it is so. There are any number of books and courses available teaching these techniques. Yet the fact is that they mostly seem to work very poorly for most people. Thought is not creative, it is the vehicle for the creativity of context. Whether visualization or affirmation techniques work for a given person depends on the degree to which the context from which that person operates his or her life allows for success. It is not that such techniques are wrong or worthless in themselves but rather that, without the grasp of the context in which they are used, we only have a part of the picture.

How, then, do we go about creating a new context? How does John, with his context of lovelessness, to take a specific example, go about creating a context of satisfying and abundant love?

The first thing—and this is what stops a lot of people dead right away—is to be clear about, accepting of and complete with, the context that we already have, that we have created unconsciously. When we do that, we automatically begin to withdraw energy from it—the energy that we are putting into maintaining it. It means starting in the middle, starting from where you actually are. You can't go back to the beginning and decide to do it differently, though that is the assumption and indeed the overt message of most, if not all, forms of therapy.

Living one's life is a matter of experiencing whatever is there to be experienced at the moment it is being experienced. That doesn't mean succumbing to it. People are often afraid that if they allow themselves to experience what's going on with them they won't be able to function. As we have already noted, everyone has a layer of negative and painful feelings that is usually kept out of consciousness. One of the big illusions that keeps us stuck is the belief that we shall be at the mercy of these feelings if we acknowledge them. The monkey mind has an infinite number of tricks for justifying holding onto the nuts and this is one of them. People have occasionally said to me things like, "I can't afford to confront my feelings because I have a job to do or children to look after, and if I let my feelings take over I wouldn't be able to do that."

In this sort of circumstance, what is actually going on is that they are doing their job *and* being aware of potentially threatening feelings. This is what they have to acknowledge and experience in order to move on. It is so obvious yet we are almost totally unable to see the obvious. I sometimes think that the reason astrology is so obsessed with trying to predict the future is that it is much easier to see the future than to see the present!

It seems unnatural, against every instinct, that, faced with unhappy feelings or circumstances, the way out is to go with them, yet, by taking responsibility for the circumstances, by aligning ourselves with what actually *is*, we reclaim the power to control those circumstances. In the early days of flying, pilots didn't know what to do when the aircraft stalled and went into a spin. The seemingly natural thing to do was to resist the spin, to try to force the aircraft to rotate against the direction of the spin. But this was a recipe for disaster. Fighting the spin increased it and the aircraft crashed. The problem wasn't solved until someone thought of doing exactly the opposite and going with the spin. In terms of the create-maintain-destroy cycle, by aligning himself with what was actually so, the pilot allowed the cycle to complete itself and the spin was eventually destroyed. Consciously or not, he was operating from a context of mastery of the condition of spinning rather than from a context of being the victim of it.

You cannot go back and start again. What you can do is to allow the contexts of your life to complete their cycles and then you have the space to create new ones that will support your self-expression in the world instead of damaging it. But it is not easy; we have the monkey mind to contend with, and it will do everything it knows in order to justify continuing to hold on to those nuts which it thinks it must have to survive. A very potent way in which it pulls us off beam is by creating the illusion that we could be doing something else other than what we are actually doing. Or feeling or thinking something else and generally being some other way than the way we are.

The power of context exists NOW, in this moment of NOW, yet what is NOW? A second? A tenth of a second? A millionth of a second?

Some fundamental particles have lifetimes which are measured in terms of 10^{-18} seconds, that is with seventeen zeros after the decimal point, and there is at least one particle that is known to have an even shorter lifetime. Such spans of time are totally inconceivable to the human mind, yet there is a point at which the particles exist NOW.

It seems that NOW is not related to time as we think of it, and the illusion that we could be some other way than the way we are NOW depends on the illusion that NOW is defined by time. Again, the issue becomes obvious when we start to look clearly at it, and again it seems at first sight too trivial to have any value or significance.

It is vital to get clear that the experience of NOW does not take place in time, otherwise the truth that we cannot be any way other than the way we are may become too frightening to confront. I'm aware that it *sounds like* saying that you can't be any other way than you are—*ever*. It sounds as though I'm saying that you've just got to make the best of it and put up with your limitations and frustrations. In terms of the spinning airplane analogy, I'm saying, recognize that you're in a spin so that you can move through it and do something that's more fun and more expansive.

If you were actually at the controls of an airplane that was spinning to earth at a hundred miles an hour, it is unlikely that you would be thinking that you would rather be at the movies or making love or that you should be doing the laundry or cleaning the car or whatever. You would be so focused on the immediacy of the situation that you would be a hundred per cent present in it. Even if you were paralyzed with fear, you would be a hundred per cent present. At that point it would be abundantly clear to you that you had absolutely no choice but to be where you were. It is this quality of being a hundred per cent present that I want to get clear about because it is the key to creating new contexts for our lives.

Such moments of intense focus do not occur very often in the lives of most of us. The situation doesn't have to be an unpleasant one. Any powerfully exciting sensation will focus us in the NOW, and while it lasts we are a hundred per cent present and we feel fully alive. A lot of people go around looking for exciting sensations to do it to them. This is why sex and high-risk sports are so popular. Ultimately, it doesn't work to do this because it amounts to coming from a position of looking to circumstances to make you feel alive, and only you have the power to make you feel fully alive.

The way to create a new context for your life is first to choose fully to be the way you are NOW. If you do this, you are aligning yourself with the truth of what is. The truth is that you don't have any other choice but to be the way you are NOW. We know this when we are highly focused by a powerful sensation, but for most of the rest of the time we have the illusion that there are all sorts of other possibilities open to us and this stops us from focusing ourselves in the NOW and so being in touch with our power of creation. I cannot be doing anything else NOW than writing these words. Five seconds ago I was looking out of the window. Two minutes from NOW I might be drinking a cup of coffee. When I am looking out of the window, I have no choice but to be looking out of the window and when I am drinking coffee, I have no choice but to be drinking coffee. But my mind, that crazy monkey, throws up all sorts of images and distractions, trying to persuade me that I should be drinking coffee when I am writing and that I should be writing when I am drinking coffee. And this is what makes us so powerless, that prevents us from being aware of our responsibility for our lives and prevents us from knowing who we really are.

Using concrete examples like writing and drinking coffee helps to make the point, but these are fairly obvious and it is at least fairly easy to discover what we are doing. On deeper levels, we do our best to stay unconscious of what we are doing or being. As long as John is operating out of his context of lovelessness at any given moment he is being a loser with women, even though he may be acting like a winner. When he accepts that he is a loser he is in a space to create being a winner. It is a paradox; it makes no sense to the mind. It goes completely against the received wisdom about life, yet it works.

A clear and classic example of it is a girl who had been struggling for a long time to overcome—as it happens—precisely this sense of detachment and distance from people that we have supposed in the case of the hypothetical John. She eventually reached a point of deciding that the truth about her was that she really *was* a cool and detached person and found that she almost immediately broke through into a new level of warmth and ability to be close to others. As I've said before, it is not easy. It takes considerable courage and clarity to see the obvious, to see what is actually so about ourselves. It is very nearly impossible to do it alone. This is where I see the tremendous value and power—or at least potential value and power—of astrology. The basic themes of our lives are clearly stated in the birth chart and so astrology can be a very effective tool for getting a client to take the first step to liberation from his or her patterns—that of being clear about what is actually so NOW. I hasten to add that the information available from the chart needs to be used with skill and compassion and not like a sword or a sledgehammer, but this is an issue that we shall be dealing with in the chapters on counseling.

The only choice that we have is to choose to be what we are and to have what we've got NOW. Anything else is an illusion that the mind creates to justify holding on to the nuts, to keep us stuck in the maintenance phase of the cycles that we have created.

I have talked about creating a new context for our lives, but that is not perhaps a very accurate way of putting it. As we become clear about and take responsibility for the contexts of limitation that we have created, we *discover* that the ultimate context from which we come is one of love, joy and capability. We don't "transcend our charts" in the sense of becoming something completely different from what the chart indicates. Rather, we create for ourselves the option of consciously and fully living our charts instead of being stuck in a limited and mechanical experience of them.

The first step is to be able to look at our lives in really black and white, specific terms and not in the kind of vague generalities that the mind prefers to deal in. When the girl in the example above was able to say "What's so for me is that I am cool and detached," she was able to move on. Usually we are stewing around in a mess of something like, "I seem to be pretty cool and detached but I don't really want to be but maybe I do want to be because you can't trust people anyway but all the same there is a part of me that's warm and loving really though I probably shouldn't let anybody know because they won't be able to handle it and anyway who needs all that hassle...." And so on to infinity. This is mind stuff. The mind can produce it a steady twenty-four hours a day without stopping for breath.

When you nail it down to specifics, you're in business. In the next chapter, we shall look at using the chart to extract the basic themes of the life and to nail the mind down to specifics.

5

Structuring Chart Interpretation

We can now begin to define and get clear about the purpose of an astrological counseling session considered within the framework of the ideas put forward in this book: it is to assist the client to become clear about the major themes of his life and to discover which of those themes have the status of context and which have the status of content; or, in terms of the magnetic field analogy, to see which of the themes of the chart equate with the secondary fields of the needles and which with the overall controlling field. The whole point of being willing to be responsible for the context of one's life—for the overall field—is that doing so downgrades its status to that of content. It becomes just another needle.

What robs most astrological counseling of much of its power to make a difference to the client is the treatment of all the chart themes as being of equal status. Astrologers will often make statements like, "It's true you have a Venus-Saturn conjunction, which is rather emotionally limiting, but you also have a Mars-Jupiter trine, which is very fortunate and go-getting. You should concentrate on the Mars-Jupiter that you have and play down the Venus-Saturn."

It sounds plausible, but if the Venus-Saturn theme has the status of context and the Mars-Jupiter theme the status of content, then the Mars-Jupiter is in an inferior position to the Venus-Saturn. The person's initiative and enterprise will, perhaps subtly, be transformed into emotional dissatisfaction. He may be president of his company and still secretly see himself as a failure because his marriage is not working too well. Alternatively, the Mars-Jupiter theme may be context and the Venus-Saturn content. In this case, the person will automatically define love and what he or she expects from love relationships in such a way that they are perceived as successful products of enterprise and initiative. This setup could, for example, signify the Don Juan or its female equivalent. The second person may be less likely to seek counseling since, although his relationships may in fact be shallow and arid, he is unlikely to be very clearly aware of the fact because they will live up to his limited expectations of them.

One cannot be sure from the chart alone what parts of it the person is holding as context and what as content. This can only be discovered in dialogue with the client. Contexts or scripts, however, are always limiting and so the sign, house position and aspects of the Moon and Saturn will give valuable clues. I would certainly always start with the hypothesis that the chart themes involving these factors are the ones most likely to have the controlling status of context.

Diagnosis is made somewhat easier by the fact that the limiting contexts from which people are likely to be operating can be classified into three groups. These can be described by the parental injunctions "Don't think," "Don't love," and "Don't be powerful." Everyone will have at least one of these in some degree, and it is not at all unusual to find people who have all three of them. It is appropriate to remind ourselves here that these are basic survival strategies. The mind has seized on them as life-or-death ways of being in the world. Not only will it not let go of them, but it will put up all kinds of resistance to having these basic strategies brought up into the light of consciousness. As I remarked in the last chapter, nailing the mind down to black and white specifics is the essential first step, but that is far from easy. It is fairly easy for you, as an astrologer, to see what your client's mind is up to—it's there in the chart—but to present the information so that it becomes living, experienced knowledge for the client is another matter entirely. At this stage, however, we need only concern ourselves with the process of extracting the raw information from a chart in such a way that it can be used as the starting point for an exploratory dialogue with the client.

In fact, it is not so much a question of extracting the information as of organizing it. This is a basic problem that students of astrology run up against at a fairly early stage. One can learn quite quickly what the individual things in a chart *mean*, at least on a superficial level, but the difficulty is in putting it all together. A number of ways have been proposed of structuring the information as an aid to synthesizing it. Some of the most popular are: using the planets, starting with the Sun, as a basis and interpreting each one by sign, house and aspect; dividing the chart into categories like work, love, personality, etc. and interpreting the factors associated with these under the general heading and, finally, using the houses as a basis and interpreting the chart round the clock, house by house.

All these methods work well enough as a means of information display but, by themselves, they will not usually focus sufficiently clearly on the central themes of the chart. Some people use a scoring system giving points for such matters as the predominant or weakest element, whether a planet is in its own sign and so on. Such a method of displaying information can perhaps signpost the presence of certain themes, but it does not automatically synthesize them.

I have suggested earlier that it is misleading to talk about the astrologer synthesizing the chart and that the synthesis of the information from the chart only takes place within the client's experience. When astrologers talk about synthesizing a chart what they really mean is bringing the information to its highest level of organization, reducing it to its most cogent and coherent form of expression. There tends to be a good deal of mystery and obfuscation around chart synthesis but, looked at in this light, all it needs is the ability to recognize the essentials of an argument. Anybody can do it; it is a perfectly everyday faculty and does not depend on any unusual psychic or intuitive abilities. It depends on the same faculty that can recognize the basic structures of a painting, a piece of music, a play, a management problem or whatever. Intuition plays a part in it but it is mostly a matter of clear thinking.

The method by which you choose to display information from the chart doesn't really matter. However, one needs some way of organizing the material so that one can detect the underlying patterns in it. Whether one needs to continue to make such full notes in practice after becoming proficient in recognizing the themes of a chart is a matter of personal choice. My own feeling is that it is desirable. If you have your information fully prepared you can have the whole of your attention on presenting it to the client. If you don't, then some part of your attention is going to be on the chart interpretation, which could have been handled before the session began.

I am aware that many astrologers prefer to come "fresh" to the chart in the client's presence, feeling that this gives a more personal and more inspired reading. It certainly gets the adrenalin going, but on those days when you aren't feeling so good or when intuition and inspiration are not working for some reason you are less likely to do the maximum job for your client than if you have handled the purely mechanical part of interpretation ahead of time.

I am not advocating "cookbook" astrology—that is, looking up the interpretation before the session and then forcing it on the client. Astrologers who prefer to approach the chart without preliminary study will argue that a given factor, say Venus in Gemini, will not operate in exactly the same way in two different people. This is true, yet one can attach a sort of average meaning, a most-likely-manifestation, to Venus in Gemini and use it as a starting point, being prepared for the fact that the delineation you start out with may only be a ballpark position. However, I continue to be surprised at how accurate such standard delineations frequently are.

If you prefer to use a large number of small factors in chart interpretation, such as midpoint pictures, Uranian planets, asteroids, etc., then preliminary notes are virtually essential, especially if the session is to be genuine counseling and not a *tour de force* display of your chart reading skills.

In looking at interpreting a chart, one thing needs to be understood in order to avoid a good deal of subsequent confusion. It is that a chart yields information that, beyond a certain point, simply repeats itself at different levels. Students often feel that they must extract the last drop of information from a chart, but this is seldom, if ever, necessary provided the main themes of the chart are fully covered and understood.

For example, a major theme of the chart may be conservatism, a heavily focused concern with material resources. The chart may have Moon in Taurus, Sun in the 2nd house, the sign Taurus on the 4th house, Mars in Cancer and Jupiter in the 10th house. In various ways, all the factors mentioned are concerned with preserving resources. It makes for a more cogent analysis to concentrate on the theme of concern with resources than to interpret the individual factors at length without relating them to the common theme. This is especially so in the first presentation of information to a client.

This, of course, is not to say that detailed interpretation is not useful in its place, but it is better to do it as an elaboration of the broad issues rather than plunging straight into it.

There are usually around six or eight major themes in the chart and these can often, if not always, in turn be reduced to one single statement that broadly sums up the chart. This final broad statement is easier to see in some charts than in others and I don't consider it essential that it should be found. Obviously, though, if one has it, it is a help since the whole of the client's life can be put into perspective in the first few minutes of the interview—if this is desirable or appropriate. It may not be.

We can distinguish five levels of intepretation, as follows:

Level 1: The broad statement made by the chart.

Level 2: The major themes of the chart.

Level 3: Interpretation of planets in signs and houses and of major and powerful minor aspects.

Level 4: Signs on house cusps.

Level 5: Subtle minor aspects, house rulers, any additional indicators such as asteroids or Arabian parts, if these are used.

I have drawn a distinction between powerful and subtle minor aspects. The powerful minors are semi-sextile, semi-square, sesquiquadrate and quincunx. The subtle minors are the nonagen, septile, quintile and bi-quintile—plus any others that you find work for you. It seems to me that the powerful minors are pretty well as potent as the majors but that they have to be used with a much smaller orb (about 3°). The subtle minors should be noted but they do not seem to work in all charts. They seem to come into play in people who have an unusually strong sense of purpose or direction. Orbs for the subtle minor aspects should be kept within 1½°. Orb for major aspects is 8°, except for the sextile, which gets 6°.

I personally do not pay much attention to preponderance or lack of elements and qualities nor to aspect patterns such as T-squares. I don't find the indications of these significators to be particularly clear or reliable. However, this is a reflection of my particular style of thinking and is not meant to be a condemnation of their use. If you find that you get important information from them, I would suggest that, in terms of the above format, they would be Level 3.

In any case, I want to be clear that the use of the five levels is only meant to be a scaffolding to create some kind of a loose and tentative structure for the interview. It is not meant to imply any dogmatic statements about how the interview should be conducted. In the average one-shot or first time session I would expect mainly to be operating in terms of levels 1, 2 and 3 but I don't want to imply that there is necessarily a linear progression. Certainly I am not saying that the earlier levels of interpretation should be exhausted before moving on to the others.

It may sometimes be appropriate, for example, to start off by stating the broad theme, or one of the major themes, then, depending on the client's reaction, moving straight to information from levels 4 or 5. If one of the major themes has to do with relationships, again for example, it may be appropriate, after putting that to the client, to go straight to considering the sign on the 7th house and its ruler. Or, if there is a Venus-Mars septile, it may be appropriate to explore it. There is no "right" way to do it, but the structure of the five levels is useful if only because it enables one to keep a sense of proportion about the mass of information available.

To demonstrate extracting information from a chart and organizing it into themes, I am going to use the format of taking each planet in turn and delineating it by sign, house and aspects and treating the Ascendant, Midheaven and Nodes as planet-like points. As used, the format is a slightly modified version of the one taught by the Faculty of Astrological Studies in England.

It will be useful to have a chart to work with that reflects the difficulties of our hypothetical "John." For the sake of clarity of example, I have made up a chart which contains the astrological factors one would expect to find for such a person (see Fig. 1.5.1). In other words, it is an astronomically valid chart but, as far as I know, doesn't "belong" to anybody. It is calculated for June 30, 1952, 10:48 AM, BST,* London. The time has been selected somewhat arbitrarily to give an exact Sun square Saturn.

Later, we will see how the chart might be used in actually counseling "John" and also look at some real-life examples. I find it useful to think of the planets as being like engines that need a certain type of fuel, shown by the sign, and that seek to operate in certain areas of experience, shown by the house. This idea will be elaborated on later, in Section 2. It is mentioned here because it will be implicit in the wording of the interpretations.

Analysis of John's Chart

⊙ in ♋ and 10: The central energy and purpose of life needs security and a warm, nurturing atmosphere in order to operate fully and will seek experiences of social acceptance, success and status.

⊙ □ ☽: Powerful, discordant physical and emotional responses. Strong outgoing energy probably turning to stubbornness, self-centeredness. Feelings of self-worth are an issue in some way.

⊙ ☌ ♀: Affectionate, outgoing, strong emotional and sexual nature liable to turn to sentimentality and/or passivity if thwarted. Will be likely to compromise at a surface level rather than handle difficulties in relationships.

⊙ △ ♂: Courageous, enterprising, active. Considerable natural self-confidence. Strong sexual nature.

⊙ □ ♄: Strong sense of self-discipline, duty, responsibility. Little capacity for pleasure. Tendency to depression, inhibition, self-denial, self-hate. Perhaps poor physical health.

⊙ ☌ ♅: Original ideas and attitudes. Strong sense of being different. Gets overexcited, hasty, impulsive. Impatient, may lack staying power, always wanting something new.

*British Summer Time.

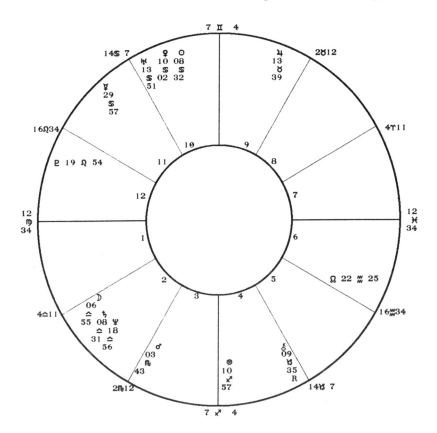

Figure 1.5.1 John. Born June 30, 1952 in London, England at 10:48 A.M., B.S.T., Greenwich. The chart was calculated using Topocentric houses. This data was invented to create a sample chart for our discussion. Calculations by Astro-Computing Services.

☽ in ♎ and 2: Drive to create a safe support system needs harmony and satisfying relationships in order to operate. Amiable, diplomatic, friendly, reasonable. It will seek expression through experiences of self-worth, possessions, stability. There is great need to be liked and enmity is difficult to handle. At the same time, automatic self-assertion leads to both outer and inner conflicts.

☽ □ ♀ : Affectionate, sensitive, gentle. Feelings usually gain the upper hand. Strong sexual, sensual nature. Sympathetic, compassionate. Tendency to become passive and victimized.

☽ BQ ♃: A potential for being social, outgoing, confident. May become involved in spiritual or religious activities or interests as a way of seeking security.

☽ ⚹ ♄: Cautious and careful in expressing feelings, though not necessarily opinions. Feelings of inferiority, inadequacy. Tendency to depression, difficulties in relationships. Tends to be private and withdrawn. Feelings seem frozen below a certain level. Prefers order, structure, routine in life.

☽ □ ♅: Can be creative and inventive but with much tension. Inclined to emphasize the differences between himself and others. Inclined to be aloof, defensive, moody.

☽ ∠ ♇: Very emotional and intense, though perhaps not overtly so. Strong desire to control emotional responses, with much blocked energy. Tends to distrust free flow of feelings.

☿ in ♋ and 11: Gaining knowledge and communicating needs emotional security in order to function. Thinking is very personal, much influenced by feelings. Makes decisions by hunch rather than by logic. Communication seeks expression through group activities, involvement with others in a nonemotional way. Ideas will operate better in team work rather than individual effort. (Some writers would say that, with Mercury being so close to the cusp, one would expect an additional Leo effect. I prefer to ignore any cuspal effects and to take sign boundaries as indicating a quantum jump.)

☿ □ ♂ : Rapid and/or forceful in speech and thinking. Irritable, witty, extremely restless. May be hypercritical, perhaps sarcastic or satirical.

♀ in ♋ and 10: Love and friendship drive needs deep feeling of emotional security in order to function. Considerate and caring in relationships, romantic, inclined to hold on too tightly. Love seeks expression through experiences of social approval. The expression of love will be intense, passionate and nurturing but outwardly will seem reserved and conformative.

♀ △ ♂ : Potentially an easy flow of emotional and sexual energy. Can be very active, demonstrative, affectionate. Love and sex are major issues in some way. (The aspect is wide, almost at the limits of the allowable orb of 8 degrees, and it may be assumed that the expression of it will be somewhat fragmentary and diluted.)

♀ ✱ ♃: Ability to be charming, generous, sociable, popular but will have to make some conscious effort to express these qualities. Basically warm-hearted, but may be underlying feeling of never being satisfied and so always in pursuit of some imagined happiness. Also, though, a genuine talent for pleasure and happiness.

♀ ☐ ♄: Tends to be cautious and defensive in relationships, to feel inadequate, rejected. Inhibition of creative impulses, perhaps renunciation or avoidance of parenthood. May dislike being touched; finds it difficult to accept compliments or other show of approval or affection.

♀ ☌ ♅: Can be very excitable, wanting drama and sensation in relationships, but energy is also subject to sudden turn-offs. Can be very friendly but without much intimacy or commitment.

♀ N ♇: Potential of a very strong, transformative sexual expression, but this is something that needs to be worked on and developed at a fairly deep level. Unlikely to be obviously manifesting.

♂ in ♏ and 3: Drive to take direct action needs intensely passionate, sexual motivation, with secrecy and inner strength. Can be ruthless, humorless, somewhat paranoid. It will seek expression through experiences of communicating and gaining knowledge. Tremendous emotional power which can be formulated into ideas and expressed in speech or writing.

♃ in ♉ and 9: Drive to grow and assimilate needs a good sense of substance and resources in order to operate and will seek experiences of growth through social involvement, religious or philosophical interests. There is a sort of permanent forward momentum here. Given some basic stability and resources, growth will lead to more growth which will lead to more resources and stability.

♃ BQ ♄: Potential for success in patient, cautious, conservative ways. May be able to make much of small opportunities.

♃ ✱ ♅: Quick grasp of situations to own advantage, desire for growth through inner development. Intuitive, but may be too dogmatic and stubborn about his intuitions.

♃ ☐ ♇: Desire for power and leadership. Usually sincere and frank, perhaps to the point of being brusque and blunt. Needs to do things in a big way.

♄ in ♎ and 2: Drive to set limits and boundaries needs harmonious, cooperative relationships in order to operate and will seek expression through experiences of self-worth and personal resources. In other words, the tendency will be to be serious, courteous and observant of form in relationships rather than very outgoing or emotional. Personal resources will be *experienced* as being inadequate and insufficient, whether they are in reality or not.

♄ □ ♅: Much inner stress and tension, constant striving to break out of set patterns yet, at the same time, wanting to maintain them. Great capacity for endurance but probably tries to do too much and so adds to tension.

♅ in 10: The drive for extraordinary insights seeks expression through experiences of status and social approval. Liable to unusual, perhaps dramatic or sensational, experiences in career and general sense of belonging to a group.

♅ □ ♆*: Tendency to be impractical, other-worldly, lacking drive and physical vitality. Capacity for intuitive understanding, compassion. Easily thrown off course by new developments.

♆ in 2: Drive for all-inclusiveness seeks expression through experiences of self-worth, personal resources. Sense of self-worth likely to be confused with a sense of unattainable standards to be met, though these will be vague.

♆ ⚹ ♇*: Capacity for self-sacrifice, intense pursuit of unusual goals and ambitions. Concern with inner exploration.

♇ in 12: Drive for complete transformation seeks expression through experiences of solitude, deprivation, inner strength. In practice, until some awareness is gained, there will be virtually a compulsion to experience this kind of restriction.

☊ in 6: Associations with others will seek expression through routine work, behind the scenes in a supporting rather than a leading role.

☊ ⚷ ☉: Relationships are an issue in some way. Able to cooperate readily or, alternatively, always at odds with colleagues. May be a feeling of inner superiority.

---

*These aspects have been interpreted for the sake of completeness but, in general, aspects between outer planets should not be given much weight as they are long-lasting, like the outer planets in signs. The Neptune-Pluto sextile is present in all charts from 1942 into the 21st century so generally it will be more characteristic of the time period than the individual. In this chart it is echoed and supported by the much more personal Pluto in the 12th house, and we may suppose that John has some access to the personal use of the energy of the sextile.

♌ ⬜ ☽: Places very emotional value on relationships, sometimes inappropriately, clinging to relationships that have served their purpose. Sentimental, nostalgic.

♌ ⬜ ♀: Pleasant, companionable and friendly but not willing to make much effort to sustain contact if own feelings are not engaged. Tends to measure contacts by their sexual potential.

♌ ⬜ ♄: Tends to be cautious and reserved with others but will take any responsibilities very seriously once they are incurred. Liable to feel inadequate and inferior in groups.

♌ △ ♆: Can be vague and idealistic about groups and associations, expecting more from them than they can deliver, leading to disappointment.

♌ ☍ ♀: Charisma, inspiring leadership, able to be in touch with a satisfying, inspiring way of living and to present this to people at large.

☋ in 12: Tendency to fall back automatically into isolation and withdrawal, especially as ♌ has so many difficult aspects.

Asc ♍: Characteristic way of presenting the self is modest, deferential, with tendency to be critical of self and others if standards of behavior are not met.

Asc ✳ ☉: Confident, individualistic demeanor. Great need to be recognized and looked up to by others. If the outgoing energy of this aspect is blocked, there may be a tendency to passive self-dramatization, e.g. moods or illness.

Asc ∠ ☿: Inclined to be talkative, may use words as a smokescreen for feelings or as a weapon. May be nervous, indecisive.

Asc ✳ ♀: Affectionate, graceful, cultured. May be inclined to strike poses. Needs a secure, harmonious atmosphere to function well.

Asc S ♂: Deep desire to push beyond his recognized limits with the feeling that he has to do it on his own and with will power only.

Asc △ ♃: Open, expansive, takes an interest in other people. Generous with his time and energy. Readily finds common ground with others.

Asc ✳ ♅: High energy, very active, excitable. Not very aware of others and seems a little aloof and unapproachable.

MC ♊: Awareness of self in relation to others is of being logical, intellectual, knowledgeable, not very emotional.

MC ⚹ ☉: Ambitious, probably highly skilled and capable but may be self-centered and perhaps patronizing. Fairly self-aware.

MC △ ☽ : Tends to maneuver towards objectives rather than go for them directly. Protective, wants to take care of others. Somewhat easily discouraged, at least temporarily.

MC ⊻ ♀ : Considerable social skill, able to turn on the charm, generally friendly and sociable. May tend to rely on charm rather than make much effort for himself.

MC △ ♄ : Cautious, prefers to work through well-established methods and procedures and to consolidate each step before moving on. May be ambitious for status and power though experiences a great deal of frustration.

MC Q ♀ : Capable of sustained and focused effort even in the depths of discouragement. May be something of a crusader.

♎ on 2: Self-worth and the experience of having personal resources depend on harmonious relationships and pleasant environment. Note position of Venus.

♏ on 3: Thinking and communicating influenced by intense, passionate feelings, often at unconscious level. Note positions of Mars and Pluto.

♐ on 4: Sense of security and personal identity is maintained by a philosophical approach to life, dependence on accepted codes of behavior. Note position of Jupiter.

♑ on 5: Creative self-expression is tailored to fit social norms. It is purposeful and calculated rather than spontaneous. Note position of Saturn.

♒ on 6: Personal adjustment, routine work, service to others are done from a need to act as part of a group. Note positions of Saturn and Uranus.

♓ on 7: Personal relationships are conditioned by the need for romance, self-sacrifice, beauty. Note positions of Jupiter and Neptune.

♈ on 8: The experience of deep sharing of energy with others or deep self-discovery depends on spontaneous self-assertion and action. Note position of Mars.

♉ on 9: The experience of having a workable philosophy of life, moral beliefs and social wisdom depends on a sense of stability, personal resources and self-worth. Note position of Venus.

♋ on 11: Experience of being a functioning member of a group and participating in group activities depends on feeling nurtured and emotionally supported. Note position of Moon.

♌ on 12: Isolation, withdrawal, experience of frustration or confinement has a quality of self-dramatization and searching for creative self-expression. Note position of Sun.

Discovering the Themes

We now have a pretty full display of the information which the chart provides. The reader will note that I have taken the meaning of the Node as being the drive to form relationships. Also, for the purposes of keeping the notes reasonably short, I have treated all aspects as if they had the same meaning. That is, I have regarded the fact that two planets are in aspect as more important than the nature of the aspect. The meaning of the nature of the aspect would be considered at a later stage if it were necessary.

From this mass of information, some of it contradictory, the basic themes emerge. The main ones are as follows:

1. Very strong, passionate feelings which require a good deal of security and support in close relationships for them to be expressed. Brooding, injured pride.
2. Severe sense of inadequacy and limitation with strong drive to cover it up by being agreeable, optimistic, courteous and sociable and by making valuable contributions to group activities.
3. Sense of scarcity of opportunity largely because of need to submit personal feelings to social *mores*. Always an underlying ambition and struggle to achieve.
4. An extremely bright, original and magnetic streak with a deep drive to clear up the problems in his life.
5. Marked tendency to withdrawal, alternately accepting the challenges set by relationships and refusing them.
6. A willingness to play the role of "victim" but with much resentment at the inhibiting of personal expression.
7. Ideas and opinions strongly held and sometimes forcefully expressed but not very readily. May be angry fantasies.

We can combine and condense these themes further into a single broad statement.

A bright, warm, outgoing person who needs a great deal of personal love and security in order to express himself and who is unable to get this love and security because of a deep-rooted sense of unworthiness and powerlessness.

With the broad statement, the major themes and the full notes we have a framework of information within which we can begin a counseling interview with John. The operative word is "begin." All of the above information is to be treated as representing a preliminary position until it is validated in John's own experience. The session is a joint endeavor, a joint process of discovery. Good counseling simply cannot be done from the viewpoint of the astrologer who feels that he has to astonish and impress his client with the accuracy of his chart reading. Some readers may initially experience that statement as threatening but, in fact, it makes life a great deal easier if you are not coming from a position of how right you are.

So far, we have said nothing about the place of predictive techniques in this type of counseling. As the emphasis is so much on having the client discover and experience the patterns of the natal chart, I see predictive techniques merely as providing supplementary information to that end. They are, nevertheless, useful and, before we get down to the specific issues of counseling, we will take a look at predictive work.

6

Prediction:
Time-Potential Indicators

In a sense, coming from the context of creating and being responsible for one's life and seeing it all as an endless dance of create-maintain-destroy processes makes prediction unnecessary, even undesirable. Since the truth is that we can only handle our lives NOW there is not really much point in speculating about what we shall be having to handle in six months' or a year's time. Predictive techniques do, however, provide further information. What they provide is information on what areas of the chart and what themes of the life are being activated at a given time.

For the most part, we are so unconscious of what is going on with us and so resistant to taking a clear look at it that we need all the external guidance and reassurance that we can get, in practice.

There is probably more confusion about the use of prediction than in any other area of astrology. To make any real sense of it we need to recognize that we create what will happen just as much as we create what *is* happening. Moreover, what will happen is entirely subject to the overall context from which we operate our lives. Though they might not have put it in just those terms, the older astrologers seem to have been much clearer about that than many astrologers today. Older books state that nothing can come about that is not shown in the natal chart, and it is stressed that one has to know the meaning of the natal chart thoroughly before even attempting to predict.

There seems to be something of a tendency today to ignore this basic rule. Partly, I suspect, this is because of pressure from clients who want to be told that their "luck" is going to change. Partly, it is because many astrologers, confronted with the seeming intractability of human nature and a difficult chart, do not know how to handle it and, understandably, seek to give comfort to their clients by dwelling on positive-seeming transits and progressions. I am not arguing that this is necessarily wrong. If a client is in a space where he or she can only hear reassurance that things will be better in a few months when Jupiter trines the Sun, it would be cruel to withhold that reassurance. It may, after all, assist him to face the immediate future with more confidence than he would otherwise have had. Someone once said to me about this kind of predictive work, "You don't really believe it and it doesn't come true but at least it makes you feel better at the time!"

Doing this kind of thing is, in TA terms, a Nurturing Parent to Child transaction. It is the equivalent of saying to a small child, "Don't worry, you'll feel better in the morning." If he believes you, he may actually feel better. Even if he doesn't believe you, the mere fact that you understand him and care enough to want him to feel better will have some positive effect. In the case of an astrologer-client relationship, it is extremely unlikely that the astrologer has anything like the power of suggestion available to an actual parent dealing with an actual child. Nevertheless, some quantity of love and caring can be transmitted to the client. If that is all that can be done, it is far better that the client should come away feeling even slightly nurtured than not nurtured at all.

There are two problems with this kind of transaction. The first and worst is that the client is not really benefited very much and certainly not permanently. The second problem is that often the reassurance is false because the astrologer doesn't really believe the prediction himself and may be as much concerned with soothing his own scared Child as with his client's. The whole thing is like whistling to keep your spirits up—not to be despised if it works!

Some astrologers, of the scientific persuasion, would argue that this placebo effect is invalid and that is has nothing to do with astrology. Certainly it is not a very high nor, in the long run, very effective use of astrology, but the point is worth making here that it is more important that a client should take away some benefit from a session than that his or her problems should be fitted into a set of theoretical principles. Obviously, however, the sort of client I have described would not be a suitable candidate for the kind of counseling approach which this book is concerned with. Such a person is completely trapped in the script and is not even in a space to begin to consider that the script exists.

As a matter of fact, it is very easy to predict the future once you know the person's scripting. The future is going to be more and more of the same thing that there was in the past, with superficial variations. But who wants to tell a client that, or contemplate it in their own lives?

The whole area of prediction is extremely tricky to handle. People are so conditioned to think of it in fatalistic terms and the mind, the ever-active monkey, loves to grab hold of predictions as a way of justifying not being responsible. This is true whether the prediction is of something positive or negative. My experience with clients is that, if they are open to this kind of approach at all, it is relatively easy to get them to accept responsibility for the way they are now. But as soon as they think about the future, they flip right back into "Something out there is doing it to me."

Indeed, this backsliding is encouraged by the way in which predictive techniques are generally used by astrologers. Even those astrologers who are psychologically oriented tend to fall back on events where predictions are concerned. Or, if not actual events, they will talk in general terms about periods of stress or restriction or expansion, or whatever planet is being activated. Some may use such expressions as, "In about three months from now, your growth process calls for a period of intense activity." And the client thinks, "Oh, God, even my growth process is doing it to me!"

Transits, progressions, solar arc directions, etc., can be usefully taken as indicators of what humanistic psychologists call the growth process. They only exist in time or, at least, they depend on time in order to manifest themselves. The natal chart is often said to be a kind of frozen snapshot of a given moment of time. This sounds plausible, but it makes no sense on closer examination. Time without change is meaningless so evidently the natal chart, or rather that total context that the natal chart represents, exists outside of time. (Obviously any physical representation of the natal chart exists in time and is subject to change, if only minute and gradual chemical alterations of the ink and paper.)

It would be perfectly possible, though extremely tedious, to draw up a list of all the possible transits, progressions, solar arc directions and so on from birth to beyond probable death. These don't change either so there is a sense in which they also exist outside of time. I have suggested, in an earlier chapter, that it helps to think of the birth chart as being a pattern that one enthusiastically chooses before birth and, of course, the pattern contains all the "predictive" elements as well.

The future is just as much a part of the total context of our lives as is the past and the present. It is as though each person's life is a complete, four-dimensional unit and it has to be immersed in space-time for it to work. Again, the analogy of a play is useful. We can hold a play that we know well as a whole. The ending and all the intermediate events in

Hamlet are implicit in the first words, yet the play itself needs two or three hours of time and a certain amount of space to act out.

The great difficulty about talking about it is, of course, that we can only do so in space-time. I have to use linear thoughts and word patterns so that it sounds as though the whole process were a time-bound one. The way I have written the description of choosing our lives before birth, with all the events and developments implicit in them, sounds fatalistic. But this is entirely because of the limitations of time-bound language. It only *looks* as though we choose the script before birth. In reality, we choose it NOW. The choice is going on compulsively outside of space and time NOW. And it is NOW that we have the opportunity to acknowledge that choice, to take responsiblity for it and to be willing to let go of it and so create the space to choose something else other than more and more of what we had in the past.

The underlying assumption of all (as far as I know) astrological prediction is that there is an objective universe, separate from us, and that it does things to us. It rewards us or punishes us or neglects us altogether, sometimes seemingly as a logical result of our actions, sometimes apparently arbitrarily. Along with this is the notion (not always very clearly stated) that, if we know in advance what the universe is going to do to us, we can somehow turn its machinations to our advantage or, at least, bear the blows philosophically when they arrive. Talking in terms of the unfolding of a growth process doesn't really alter this. It sounds more dignified and humane but it still leaves us in the position that the power in our lives is in the growth process. It sounds enlightened to talk about our growth process calling for a period of restriction rather than talking about Saturn giving us hell right now, but in doing that we are creating a Frankenstein monster which we can see we have created but which is now on an unstoppable rampage of its own. We are not really any better off than with the more obviously naive view that Saturn up there has his beady eye on us and we'd better watch out.

In terms of taking responsibility for our life so that we can recreate it consciously, the current use of astrological prediction is misleading, misguided and downright oppressive in that it encourages belief in and dependence on some external power or process. As we have seen, the natal chart contains certain potentials which "eventually" manifest in the space-time world. These potentials are indicated by the familiar prediction techniques, and prediction as it is currently used consists of using one's knowledge of the time potentials of the chart to speculate about the future, sometimes accurately and sometimes not, in a way that caters to the monkey mind and draws attention away from the potentially liberating NOW.

In saying this, I don't want it to be construed as an attack on astrologers who use prediction—a category that includes many people who have my greatest affection and respect. What I am really saying is that, if you want to use astrology as a tool for liberation and enlightenment you cannot, logically, use prediction in the form of speculating about the future. As I have pointed out at the beginning of this chapter, there are other uses of astrology which are also valid within their own terms and within which prediction does have a part to play.

It is really a matter of being clear about the way you are using astrology and of what is appropriate. Nothing could be less appropriate than ramming the notion of being responsible for one's life down the throat of a client who is not at the point of being willing to make that assumption, and who will experience your insistence on it as a cold rejection of his or her problems and needs. After all, you have created that client in your experience and it is up to you to do what needs to be done in order to benefit him. If what needs to be done is to do some predictions, then so be it.

So, do these time potentials of the chart have a use in what one might call transformational astrology? They do, but it is a much less important one than they have in traditional event oriented astrology or in humanistic, growth-process oriented astrology. We constantly create opportunities for ourselves to become aware of and responsible for the contexts from which we operate our lives, and we can use current transits, progressions and solar arc directions to become clearer about the nature of the opportunities that we are creating. As I have said earlier, if we were able consistently to come from a clear experience of responsibility for our lives, it wouldn't be necessary to use these time-potential indicators in this way. It wouldn't be necessary to do the basic astrological analysis either. As it is, with the mind generating so much confusion and resistance as it insists on being right and holding on to the basic script, we can use all the aids to clarity that we can get.

Before using the time-potential indicators—a term I will use in preference to "predictive techniques"—it is essential to have a clear understanding of the basic issues in the life as shown by the natal chart and as clarified in interaction with the client. The client will always come in with an issue which is a specific manifestation of the generalized context, and which constitutes an opportunity for him to gain clarity both about the specific manifestation itself and the general underlying context. The client may not—in fact usually does not—know what the issue is, and it is a major goal of the session to identify it, as we shall see later in following chapters on counseling. Sometimes current transits will point clearly to the issue.

An example is that of a person with Sun in Aries, Mars conjunct Saturn in Leo, Jupiter sesquiquadrate Saturn, Venus in Taurus opposite the Moon. In the session, it became clear that the major specific issue was a compulsive material striving, powered by a fear of poverty and of losing all the resources that she had. This was established entirely from the natal chart and mainly from the significators that I have quoted. Once this was clear and the client was at the point of being willing to accept and be responsible for this pattern of fearful striving, it was useful to look at the current transits for further information. These were: Pluto-T quincunx Venus, Neptune-T quincunx Venus, Jupiter-T opposite Sun and Saturn-T opposite Sun.

These can be interpreted as: self-worth, inner resources, support given and received, and basic sense of identity (Venus opposite Moon) are being subject to a drive for a total reassessment (Pluto), and much vague fear, confusion and uncertainty (Neptune). At the same time, the central sense of wanting to be in the world (Sun) was being stimulated by drives both for growth and assimilation (Jupiter) and a strong sense of apparently necessary limitations (Saturn). This further information enabled her to get in touch with and clarify the feelings that she had around these issues.

This is a slightly unusual example in that the transits and other timing indicators do not often show the specific issue as clearly as they did in this case. I see the use of timing indicators in this way as having a twofold value. First, they can provide further clarity about what is going on and, second, they validate what is going on. It gives a reassurance to the client that the position he is in and the feelings he is experiencing are in fact exactly the position and the feelings he is *supposed* to be experiencing so that he can confront them and allow them to process out. The difference between this and saying that it's all part of the growth process is subtle but crucial in that the emphasis is put firmly on the client's responsibility for creating current circumstances as well as the general life pattern.

There still remains the question of whether there is any value in giving information ahead of time. I think the answer to this must depend on the individual client. If the client is someone who is following some kind of spiritual or psychological program and is really committed to being responsible for his or her own life, it can be useful to give some general pointers about the issues that will be emphasized in future periods. In that way, the client has information that he can use *at the time* that the transits, etc. are having an effect in his life. In other words, one can say something like, "In about three month's time such and such an issue will be highlighted in some way. If you look at what's going on with you then in the light of this information, you may find it helps you to become clearer about it." But even putting it in these terms is an invitation to the monkey mind. If it can persuade us to put something off into the future it will do so. With any kind of forecasting, there is a great temptation to think in terms of reserving ourselves for when the transit arrives and so being distracted from what we need to do NOW.

My general practice, at the moment, is not to volunteer information about future trends. Since the whole point of the session is to assist the client to get to a place where he can create his own future, it is not helpful to talk as though the future had something "in store" for him. If he specifically asks for information about future trends, I usually gently discourage him, drawing attention to the fact that it is the mind that wants to know and not the Real Self. There are two main exceptions to this. One is the case mentioned above where I sense that having the information is going to assist the client to take responsibility for his life at those later dates. The other is where the client is about to start on some new venture and is concerned or anxious about it. The cardinal rule is still *always* first to identify the script patterns and look at the venture in that light. But if there are important time-potential indicators operating around the date of the projected venture, having information about them ahead of time may again assist the client in gaining clarity and responsibility for what is going on when the time comes.

There is a third exception; I will sometimes give future information if it seems intuitively right to do so in the general context of the session. Each session is individual and one cannot entirely be bound by hard and fast rules. But, in general, I aim to get through the session without talking about the future at all.

Predicting in specific terms is difficult in any case. Sometimes major transits, solar arcs or progressions go by without any noticeable effect, either inner or outer. At other times, major events occur which apparently have no astrological correlates. In the first instance one may suppose that the person is so unready to confront the issues indicated that they are seemingly not activated at all. I have known such an apparently major indication as progressed Sun conjunct Mars pass without any detectable manifestation whatever. There was a strong basic scripting to withdrawal and passivity which was very much in the forefront of the client's life at the time. In the second case, one can almost always find an astrological correlate after the event, if one looks hard enough. But it is not always the sort of thing one would look for before the event. A case that comes to mind is that of a man who suddenly made the most drastic change in every area of his life. He gave up his marriage, family, profession and native country to live in comparatively reduced circumstances with a woman he had fallen in love with. The only indicator of all this was that progressed Sun was conjunct the Mars-Uranus midpoint. This configuration is certainly appropriate to the event but few astrologers would have looked for it in doing a routine scan for the purposes of prediction.

Taking responsibility for one's life and, therefore, being willing for the create-maintain-destroy cycles to be complete, does actually and literally destroy a part of the script, however small a part it may be. If this happens during the counseling session—and it is my intention that it should—the client is literally not the same afterward. He or she has gained some measure of freedom from the script. It may be a tiny measure, to be thought of in terms of a pinprick compared with the script mechanism as a whole, but it is there and the script structure has been weakened. The probability is, therefore, that he will not respond to time-potential indicators in the same way as he would if the session had not occurred. This, again, makes any form of prediction hazardous. The better job you do the more likely the client is to "use" his chart in different ways, which will not become apparent for some time. So the basis on which you would have predicted has changed in ways you cannot know during the session.

In summary, my view of the value of time-potential indicators is that, if the client has a reasonable degree of clarity about his script patterns, they are not really necessary. They can, however, be useful if used in the present time to gain more clarity about what is going on at that time and to relate it to script patterns and so become more conscious of the ramifications and subtleties of the script patterns.

Of the three types of timing indicator that I have mentioned, transits seem to me to be the one that works most consistently and clearly, with solar arc directions a good second and secondary progressions a rather poor third. Until fairly recently, I calculated all transits, solar arcs and secondary progressions for the day of the session, paying attention not only to major aspects but to semi-squares, sesquiquadrates, and quin-cunxes. My current practice is to look at transits only, again paying attention to the powerful minor aspects. The reason for using transits only is purely pragmatic; they provide all the information I am likely to need in practice. Doing solar arcs and secondary progressions is a lot more work for not much extra result. (If you use a computer or a computer service, this consideration obviously does not apply so much.)

In interpreting transits—or, for that matter, solar arc directions and progressions—I give the main importance to the planet that is being aspected in the natal chart. Doing it this way makes it easier to see what script patterns are up for confrontation. Obviously, the aspecting planet and the nature of the aspect being made make a difference to the way in which the natal issue is activated, but the useful thing is the opportunity to gain awareness of the basic issues involved. Thus, if Venus is being aspected, the valuable thing is the opportunity to become more conscious of patterns and belief systems about love and personal worth. Whether Venus is being activated by a trine from Jupiter or a conjunction from Saturn is, from this point of view, much less important.

Again, in talking in this way, we are running into a language difficulty. It is hard to avoid sounding as though some outside effect were stimulating the basic issue. It is more accurate and helpful to say that the natal planet, the aspecting planet and the nature of the transiting aspect show us the basic issue and the way in which we are choosing to manifest and confront it. The transiting planet and the nature of its aspect may be regarded as the clothing or disguise that the basic issue is wearing for the time being.

Sometimes, as with the example given earlier, the same issue appears in two disguises simultaneously. Here, Venus was being aspected by Neptune and Pluto—both planets whose action is rarely clear to the reasoning mind—and both planets were making a quincunx, an aspect which itself has the nature of being disjointed and awkward. This is an extremely complex situation which can really only be handled by going to the root of the matter and noting that, in this particular case, issues of love and self-worth were up to be confronted. Similar considerations apply to the simultaneous transit of the Sun by Jupiter and Saturn.

One also needs to take the total condition of the natal planet into account. In the example, Venus is in Taurus, in the 9th house, semi-square Sun and opposition Moon. So it is not just Venus that is being activated but that whole complex. This, again, is another reason why one needs to do a thorough natal analysis before looking at time potentials.

There are a number of excellent books which delineate the likely effects of transits, but they need to be used with this consideration of the total condition of the natal planet in mind. For example, transiting Mars conjunct Moon will most likely correspond with feelings of anger, irritation, separateness from others. The basic issues underlying these feelings will, however, be very different when Mars transits a chart with, say, Moon in Aries in the 7th, square Uranus from what they are when Mars transits a Moon in Taurus in the 12th, square Saturn.

The question of how long a transit, solar arc direction or secondary progression lasts is not an easy one. Some writers advocate using an orb of 1° before and after the transit is exact. Others reduce this to ½°; others again, notably Ebertin, say that the point of exactitude marks the effective end of the transit and that it should only be considered for the time the planet takes to travel 1° to the exact aspect.

If we are talking about events, these rules are appropriate. A time-potential indicator stirs up the issues shown by the natal planetary complex and this activity may or may not manifest as an external event. If it does so manifest, it is most likely to do so when the aspect is exact or very nearly exact. There are exceptions to this. Aspects involving Saturn, whether as the aspecting planet or the natal planet, are inclined to produce an appropriate event some time after exactitude. This is a well-recognized phenomenon. Less well recognized is that transiting Pluto often seems to produce an event long before one would expect it—when still 3° or more from exactitude. Generally speaking, however, the small orbs apply. My own inclination is to use the rule of +/–½° for transits and +/– 5' for solar arc directions and secondary progressions. For some reason, solar arc directions seem to be the indicators most likely to produce a concrete event and to do so within about a week on either side of exactitude. For this reason, the method is a useful tool for rectifying charts.

Some people seem much more prone to have the timing indicators manifest as events than others. It is difficult to say why this should be, but it seems at least partly to relate to the tendency for people to be split into two groups. There are those who identify most with their mental processes and those who identify most with their feelings. Mentally-identified people are less event prone. Feelings-identified people need a lot of drama in their lives and are thus more inclined to create a lot of events. A very strongly mentally-identified person can go for years without any major events of personal consequence. A very strongly feelings-identified person, on the other hand, will have a life style that consists of hurtling from one dramatic personal crisis to another.

From the point of view of having the person use what is going on to become clear about script patterns, it doesn't matter very much whether there is an event or not as long as there are some fairly strong feelings and attitudes to be confronted. It may be more difficult when there is an event to confront such feelings and attitudes because of the need to deal with the physical consequences of the event. Partly for this reason and partly in order to give oneself the maximum time to see what is going on, it seems sensible to take an orb for transits which will put them on a time scale comparable with progressions and solar arc directions. Solar arcs move at the rate of about 1° = 1 year. Progressions depend on the speed of the progressed planet and so can vary from about 1° = 9 months for Mercury to 1° = 2 years for Mars. For progressed Moon, of course, 1° = 1 month, approximately.

In her book *Transits, The Time of Your Life,* Betty Lundsted advocates using an applying orb of 10° for each transiting planet. This was a startling idea to me at first but, as I have checked it out, it has come to make a lot of sense. It is particularly useful for Mars and Jupiter transits, which are over almost before you know what's happening using the small orbs. Taking a 10° orb, of course, means that there can be a lot of transiting aspects happening at the same time, which can be confusing. I find it works best not to look for the aspect and then try to identify the feelings and attitudes, but to do it the other way round. That is, to start with what you are experiencing and see what transiting planets within a 10° orb of a major aspect can throw some light and clarity on your experience. This is most usefully done with your own chart. In looking at transits for a client for the here-and-now session I take orbs of about 5° for major aspects and 2° for minors.

Most writers assume that the effect of a transit, solar arc direction or progression ends when the aspect is exact, or shortly afterwards. In terms of the probability of an event being produced, this is so. But the way I am suggesting looking at these time-potential indicators is not that they add anything to the life but that they reveal the underlying structure that was already there. If one becomes aware of and confronts a major script pattern under the effect of, say, a particular transit, the exploring and confronting of that issue can go on for a long time after the transit is over astronomically. After all, if you have been quite unconscious of some pattern in your life for thirty or forty years, it is very unlikely that it will be resolved and cleared up in the relatively short period of a transit. In fact, if one works intelligently with a transit, solar arc or progression, it seems to me that the point of exactitude coincides with the maximum consciousness of the issue that one can attain, given one's general level of self-awareness.

In this sense, the effect of a time-potential indicator does not end until the script issue involved has been allowed to move to destruction. What does happen is that the issue ceases to be so emphasized, so much of a foreground matter in your life and, if properly handled, can be allowed to be just something that is so.

7

Counseling Framework

We now have the major themes of the life stated as simple propositions and we also have a metaphysical framework within which the information can be used in a practical way. The purpose of the counseling session is to have the client acknowledge these themes, to have him get clear on which of them has the status of context, and to have him be willing to confront them from a master context of being responsible for them. Notice particularly that I have said a master "context," not a position. A position is a mind-created condition, where the client believes in responsibility, agrees with it or disagrees with it or hopes it will work. A context, on the other hand, is a function of the Real Self. It is superior to and includes all the believing, agreeing and disagreeing and hoping.

So we can also say that the purpose of the counseling session is to assist the client to get in touch with his Real Self. As noted in the last chapter, there is always a main issue that the client comes in with, which he may or may not be conscious of and which may or may not be indicated by the current transits and progressions. As I see it, the main object of the session is to have the client get in touch with his Real Self *in relation to this main issue.* To the extent that he experiences his own power, then, it will be firmly grounded and channeled, by being directly related to a clear-cut pattern in his practical, everyday life.

Some of the information available from the birth chart will be directly related to the main issue, but a good deal of it will not. I therefore distinguish two uses of the chart information. The first is in assisting the client to get to a mini-enlightenment experience around his main issue. The second is to provide him with material which he can use later on his own. It is my practice to tape record the interview so that this information is permanently available to the client. Most sessions fall into three phases. There is a preliminary presenting of the notions about creating one's reality that form the basic framework of the session. Then there is the work with the main themes to discover which of them are contextual and to get the client to a point of clarity about what he is doing with his life. This second phase is usually an intense and concentrated interaction since it has to be done against the resistance of the monkey mind. This part of the session can well be described as using the chart information to hammer away at the mind until something breaks and the monkey lets go of the nut, if only for a few seconds. When the point of clarity has been reached, this is as much as can be done in terms of loosening the grip of the script, at least in the one session. The third phase is usually more relaxed and is a more or less straightforward giving of information for the record and for future use.

About ninety-five per cent of interviews follow this pattern but there are some that don't have a third, information-giving phase. This happens when it takes so long to get to the point of clarity against the mind's resistance that there is neither time nor energy left to do anything further. Some interviews don't even get to the point of clarity, but they are rare. If you are clear yourself about what your client's monkey mind is up to, all it usually takes to get the client clear about it is enough persistence and staying with the issue.

Let us consider these three phases in some detail. The first is the creation of the working framework, and there are three points that need to be established. The two main ones are the create-maintain-destroy cycle, with the stress on the mind's investment in being stuck in the maintain phase and the notion of everything in one's life being there by intention. The third point, that often seems useful in establishing the first two, is the idea that life is like a drama that the Real Self has chosen to star in—and has become identified with the part it is playing.

The way of presenting these notions that works is to have them be the rules of the game that you and the client are going to play for the next couple of hours. Don't ask him to believe in them or to be committed to them beyond the end of the interview. The point is rather to treat them as a scientific hypothesis and to see what value there is in assuming that they are true.

With experience, everyone will develop their own way of doing the initial presentation. I usually start off by asking the person if he is willing, for the next couple of hours, to adopt the hypothesis that, at some level, he is responsible for creating his own reality. Once you begin working in this way, clients tend to be self-selecting in the sense that they are open to this approach, and it is a long time since anyone has said "no" to this.

Sometimes I put it as a statement rather than as a question and say some such thing as, "For the next couple of hours, I want us to come from the assumption that there is a level at which we actually and literally create our personal reality." Then, without giving the client time to react one way or the other, I talk about how we seize on certain ways of being in the world as survival mechanisms in very early childhood. I then explain that these childhood decisions or choices become unconscious but nevertheless go on running our lives—the more powerfully, in fact, *because* they are unconscious.

At this point I describe the create-maintain-destroy cycle. I point out that problems are processes that are stuck in the maintenance phase of the cycle and that they can be released by being clear about them and taking responsibility for them. I will bring in the analogy of the monkey who is stuck because he won't let go of the nuts. It is a striking image that most people can relate to, and it is useful to have the metaphor of the monkey to refer to later in the second phase of the session. I may bring in the notion of choosing our lives before birth at this point or I may save it for the second phase as a way of reinforcing whatever is going on then.

Though the ideas may be unfamiliar to many people, I have found that presenting them is much less difficult than one might think. If they are going to be unacceptable, I usually discover this in the preliminary conversation. Basically, either a person is interested in a depth approach or he is not. Almost invariably I have found that if the client is willing to look into his life in some depth, there is no difficulty in having him accept the framework as a working hypothesis for the session.

Sometimes a client will make it clear that he does not want any kind of depth approach but wants straightforward information about himself without any self-revelation. In such a case, I do what is asked and it usually happens that, halfway through the session, the client says, "What can I *do* about it?" At that point, one can at least introduce the ideas of childhood decisions and the create-maintain-destroy process. It can be useful to point out that this is a natural, self-healing, self-regulating mechanism.

The second stage of the interview is presenting the information from the chart with the intention of uncovering the main issue. In practice, this means that I have a written list of the main themes of the chart and I read these out as a starting point for discussion. At this stage I use no astrological terminology at all. I used to use astrological terms quite freely and explain the chart as I went along, but I am now of the view that this does not serve any real purpose and, in fact, can delay getting the client to the point of clarity. Some clients ask for the astrological references. These can be given in the third phase of the session. It is something that needs to be carefully watched since the desire for this information is usually a smoke screen from the monkey mind. Thinking and talking about your Sun square Moon or whatever can be a way of avoiding the reality—and especially the *feelings* that are part of that reality—of what it actually means in your life.

I explain that the themes as presented are "ballpark" statements, and I ask the client if they make sense to him and, if so, how they actually manifest in his life. Most clients accept most of the themes in the form that they are presented but I never insist on the specific form of a statement. On the rather rare occasion when a client does not at all recognize a chart theme, I ask if there is any way in which the general spirit of what I have said applies in his life. This almost invariably provides a formulation that we can work with. If it does not, I just drop that particular theme.

The reasons for a client not recognizing a particular chart theme are several. Often it is simply that the statement is worded in a way that doesn't connect with the way in which he would word it. Sometimes, it is because the statement comes close to something that he doesn't want to reveal. In my experience, though, clients don't usually deny such things outright. They will look uncomfortable, mutter something vague and obviously want to move on to something else. Again, even though I may sense that an important issue is being activated, I will not insist on it. Going up against that much resistance at such an early stage will only alienate the client and make the work that much more difficult.

An outright denial of a particular statement, without any obvious emotional charge on it, is most likely to happen when the chart is dubious anyway, because of an unavoidable doubt about the birth time. Ideally, all charts should be rectified but, in practice, this is impossible. Personally, I love precision and would like to work all the time with charts that are accurate to the second. In terms of getting a person to clarity and responsibility about a major issue, however, you can get the job done with a doubtful birth time or no birth time at all.(What you can't do so well, of course, is the phase three detailed information giving.)

In working in this way, it is important to get off the authoritarian, doctor-patient model of the interview and to be clear that what you are doing is a joint exploration of the client's chart and life. If the client expects to be impressed by your knowledge of mysterious occult secrets and that you will know more about him than he does, he is definitely not the right material for this approach.

The Psychosynthesis therapists have an analogy which seems to me to be very apt. It is that the therapist—or, in this case, the astrologer—is like a mountain guide. The client has hired you because he wants assistance in getting where he wants to go—not where you want to go or where you think he should go. Obviously, you know more about climbing mountains than he does but he is entitled to expect that your skill be used in his service, not in impressing the hell out of him with your ability to climb a precipice with one hand. And that image describes the position of too many astrologers who have considerable, even brilliant, interpretational skills but little sense of how to apply them within a counseling relationship. Being a virtuoso performer for every client is very hard work. Treating each session as a cooperative venture is not only likely to be more productive but is a lot easier on the nerves.

In fact, with all chart information, whether natal or time-potential indications, it is useful to take the view that you are using it to assist the client to discover what is already there, rather than that you are telling him something that he doesn't know. It is as if the client's psyche were a long-buried artifact that has just been excavated. Your job is to brush away the dirt so as to reveal the underlying structure. And the chart tells you exactly *where* to brush, which gives you a great advantage over more conventional therapists.

When you go through the major themes with the client, there will usually be at least one that obviously rings a bell. Often, this comes across as a sense of relief from the client. He may give out general signs of being particularly interested in it or he may begin to talk about it at some length; in which case, treat it as a definite lead-in to the actual work with the client. If none of the themes has this effect, pick one and ask the client to elaborate on it. None of the themes as stated is likely to be the client's own main issue. One which provokes obvious interest is likely to lead most quickly to the main issue, but it doesn't really matter where you start as long as you start somewhere.

In getting the client to talk about one or all of the themes of the chart, two things are happening. First, you are having the client relate to the statements you have made and actually owning them as a part of his experience. If he doesn't do this, the statements will remain at the level of intellectual information and have very little power. Second, you are looking for a way of encapsulating the experience he is trying to express in such a way that it registers with him on all levels—mental, emotional and physical.

The reason for attempting to encapsulate what a client is saying is to facilitate his having an experience of a context from which he is creating his life. The actual words you will use will depend on what he said specifically, but the context will always be describable in terms of one of the Transactional Analysis injunctions. The most common of these are:

Don't be close
Don't have feelings
Don't love
Don't accept love
Don't trust
Don't be sexual
Don't enjoy your body
Don't be the sex you are
Don't be yourself (always please somebody else)
Don't make it
Don't think (act stupid instead)

You may add others from your own experience, but this list is certainly enough to help develop a sense of what to look for in your clients.

As you and your client begin the dialogue which is intended to create the opportunity for him to have the experience of context, his mind will resist that experience. The resistance may take various forms but the most common are:

1. Refusing to discuss the issue at all.
2. Rationalizing and justifying.
3. Wanting the problem to be fixed instantly.
4. Denying the generality of the context.

In the case of 1, there is little you can do about it except try again from another angle. We are assuming that this has not happened since the dialogue is proceeding, but sometimes a client will show a willingness to get into an issue and then pull a switch on you. That should not happen very often but we will consider how to handle it in the next chapter.

In the case of 2, the client will get endlessly into the detail of it all. This can become the kind of compulsive retailing of events that people do in ordinary life, full of anecdotes and what she said and what I said and all the rest of it. It may look very self-revealing, especially if the anecdotes are about intimate emotional encounters, but it is at best a stage that the client must be guided through and may be a way of avoiding the experience of context altogether. This rationalizing and justifying needs patience and intuition to deal with; it is a matter of knowing when to intervene. On the one hand, you have to let the client do some of it as it is the raw material for the session, and he may need the experience of talking about himself at this level of anecdote and explanation before he can move on. On the other hand, if you don't stop it at some point, the whole session is just talk and is more or less wasted. I had one client who was so obsessed with telling me all the details that I was quite unable to control it. Not only did we not get to a point of clarity, but I was hardly able to tell him anything about his chart either. He would have been better off to have found himself a sympathetic bartender, but this was an extreme case.

Contrary to the stereotyped sexual images, I have found that it is male clients who are most likely to get into the compulsive talking. This is not so surprising since it is really a defence against being in touch with feelings, and, in our culture, men have more training against expressing or even experiencing feelings than do women. The client in question had a strong emphasis on Pisces, Scorpio and the 8th house; he may have had a catastrophic fear that he would be overwhelmed by feelings if he gave them any chance at all. With a woman, I have found that it sometimes works just to allow her to talk and she will eventually say something that brings her to tears. This stops the flow of words and is almost always an indication of a readiness to move to the next stage.

The conditions necessary for dealing with rationalizing and justifying need to be created in the first phase of establishing general principles, while the client's mind is unthreatened by specifics. Having established at that stage that we are looking for a simple statement to describe the client's life pattern and that the mind will do all that it knows in order to resist getting to that specific statement, you can pull the client back on purpose by reminding him frequently of those two facts. If the person goes off into a long and detailed explanation of a relationship, a childhood incident or job problems, I usually let him do it for a bit and then say, "All that is the monkey struggling to hold on to the nuts. What's really going on? What are the feelings that you have when you talk about it?" The person might respond, "I feel I should have done it differently," or "I feel my mother should have stayed home more often," or something similar. In this case, you have to teach your client what feelings are; that they are conditions of joy, sadness, love, pleasure, grief, anger, fear and so on. If the client has had some previous experience of therapy, you have a much easier patch to hoe.

I find it very useful, in getting through all forms of resistance, to make free use of all the analogies discussed in the earlier chapters. Thinking of context as the magnetic field which gives all the compass needles the quality of northness, or as of red goggles that fit so tightly that we don't even know that the world looks red to us, can be of great assistance in keeping the client on track. And the monkey trapping itself by holding on to nuts that it believes it must have in order to survive helps the client to recognize his resistance for what it is.

I should perhaps make it clear that I am not using the word "resistance" in the way that more conventional therapists, particularly psychoanalysts, are inclined to do. In that sense, it usually means the client's unwillingness to accept a piece of interpretation. In the sense in which I am using it, it is rather the client's unwillingness to accept himself. This unwillingness operates on two levels. First we are unwilling to accept that what is so about us *is so*, independently of our judgments about it. Second, we are unwilling to accept that in reality we are magnificent, powerful, loving, indeed godlike, beings. The mind cannot conceive of that since its sole purpose is survival in the limited space-time world. This is why it is so important to keep confronting the client with what his mind is doing. Eventually, he will "get" that he is not his mind, if only for a split second. A split second, which is actually NOW, is all that it takes to make a permanent hole in the script.

The form of resistance for 3 is wanting to fix it. This may be accompanied by an attitude of urgency and desperation. Alternatively, the client may be brisk and positive, ready to roll up his sleeves and really hack it. In either case it is more mind stuff. The mind is much trickier than any actual monkey. Typically, wanting to fix it will arise when the person has got really clear that he is running his life from a destructive belief pattern—for example, "Whatever I do, I can never make it." He may then say either, "Tell me what to *do* to get rid of this belief," in an urgent, panicky way, or "Great, now I can get rid of this stupid belief that I can't make it."

Whatever form the reaction takes, it is simply setting up another belief (I can get rid of it) in opposition to what has been discovered. The monkey is trying another trick in order to go on holding on to the nuts. The thing to do here is to point out that wanting to fix it is still part of the pattern and that it isn't *possible* to fix it in terms that the mind understands. Remind the client of the create-maintain-destroy cycle, and that what he really needs to do is to allow the cycle to process out and to allow the belief to be destroyed in the natural process of things. The way to do this is by acknowledging that the belief is there, accepting it in a nonjudgmental way, being willing to be responsible for having created and for continuing to maintain the belief, and to be willing to let go of it. It can be useful to read to the client the quotation from Jung in Chapter 1, beginning "We must be able to *let things happen* in the psyche." (My italics.)

It does seem completely contrary to the way we are normally conditioned to think of things not to attack or otherwise go against a destructive belief once it has been identified. Nevertheless, attacking it or deliberately acting in opposition to it is simply resisting it and adding to its mass. As noted in Chapter 5, this fact makes nonsense of a great deal of seemingly plausible astrological advice (Play up your Mars-Jupiter and play down your Venus-Saturn!).

Type 4 resistance denies the generality or the all-pervasiveness of the context. Let's take again the example of a context of never making it. As this begins to get exposed, the client may indignantly begin to adduce examples of occasions when he *has* made it.

The first thing to do when this happens is to consider that you might be wrong and tell your client so quite frankly. If you are genuinely unsure, then abandon that line and try another hypothesis based on one of the injunctions listed above. If your intuition is right in the first place, the conversation will come back to the never making it. (It is always a help to remember that your client's Real Self wants to have the issue cleared up even if his mind doesn't. That is what has got him into your consulting room in the first place.)

Actually, if the client indignantly denies the generality of the proposition, the indignation itself is usually an indicator that you are on the right track and are encountering resistance. In some cases it might be appropriate to confront the client quite directly with that statement. It depends on the degree of rapport that exists between you. It is safer to gently but persistently invite him to look at the examples he is producing of the times when he did make it and to see if there is anything about them that is less than totally satisfying. Eventually he will get off his defensive position about it and start to look at what is really so for him. That may not happen within the time limit of the session, and if it doesn't there may be nothing you can do but invite the client to go on looking at the issue as objectively as he can on his own.

This is another reason for giving the client a tape recording of the session. I have sometimes had people contact me months after the session and say that they have listened to the tape and heard themselves saying things that were just not so.

A striking example of someone getting off such a defensive position within the interview is that of a woman who, I thought, was operating out of a context of never getting really satisfying love. I put this to her and, with the typical indignation, she insisted that one relationship in particular had been wonderful in every possible way. Among other things, she had an exact Venus opposite Neptune, with Venus in Pisces, so I felt very confident that disappointment and self-deception in love were issues in some way. The general rapport between us was good, and she was clear about and committed to the purpose of what we were doing.

I kept inviting her to look at what there was about that relationship that had not satisfied her. Eventually she said that, although the physical and emotional content of the relationship had been wonderful, the man had not been free and they could not make a full life together. Acknowledging that brought up a lot of feeling of sadness and the recognition that never getting love in the way she wanted it was a context from which she was operating her life.

It wasn't that she consciously knew this and was deliberately not disclosing it. It was that her mind had refused to let her see the issue in such black and white specific terms before that moment.

It takes a little experience to recognize when your client has really, at all levels, "got" that he is running his life from a limited context such as the above. When you have seen it a few times it is readily recognizable but it isn't particularly easy to describe. The main characteristic of the state is that the person will look and act stunned by the perception, though this usually only lasts a few seconds. It may be followed by obvious sadness or pain, as in the above example. It is not at all uncommon for the person to see right away the absurdity of doing such a thing to himself and to burst into laughter.

Either way, ask the person if he is willing to let go of the pattern and have it clear up. The client who has laughed will probably give you a clear "yes" and mean it and you will both feel right about his reply. Even so, have him really look at the possible consequences in his life of letting go of this particular nut. He may begin making it in his life and that may mean, for example, that he will have to start dealing with internalized parental disapproval that not making it has protected him against. The client who has had the experience of context but has not lightened up very much may say "yes" to the question out of a desire to please or to fix it. Obviously, this is not a genuine "yes" and the fact will usually readily be detectable. In this case, go on pressing until you get either a genuine "yes" or a clear "no." It doesn't really matter what the answer is as long as the client is being truthful. If he is clear that what is so for him is that he is being run by a pattern of not making it and that he is not willing to give it up, the "no" will eventually turn into a "yes" if he stays with it.

This simple telling the truth about where we are in life is what works, and yet it is so difficult to do. This point of truth is usually reached in a counseling session after about an hour or an hour and a half. When it is reached a part of the script is actually destroyed. The client can never be quite the same again, if only because he can no longer be unconscious of that particular issue. I make a point of stressing this to the client so that he knows it, whether his feelings about it are high or low.

The final phase of the session is the simple giving of further information from the chart that has not been used up to that point. At this stage, there is no attempt to use it to get a result; it is intended to be for the client's future reference and use. Since contexts are so all-pervasive, the client usually makes connections with what has gone before. If, for example, the area focused on in the second phase was career problems, it is usually recognizable that the same pattern shows up in other areas, such as sex or family relationships.

8

Basic Principles of Counseling

In the last chapter we looked at the broad scheme of counseling in terms specifically of the metaphysical framework advocated in this book. In this chapter I want to consider some of the basic principles of counseling in general. These principles seem to me to be the essence of good counseling whether you use the framework of responsibility or not, and whether you do astrology or not.

First, we need to get clear about what counseling is and what it isn't. As I remarked in Chapter 1, there is a tendency among astrologers to say that they are doing counseling when all they are doing is interpreting charts and giving advice. It's not that there is anything wrong with this, but it isn't counseling and shouldn't be called by that name if we want to be clear about what we are doing. Terms like "chart readings" or "astrological consultations" can be retained for the sort of work that more or less begins and ends with the giving of accurate information. There is no reason why the same astrologer should not do a reading or a consultation on one day and a counseling session the next, depending on what is appropriate for the client. In fact, I would suggest that readers who are interested in adopting the transformational approach described here can introduce it gradually into an existing "consulting" practice.

Defining counseling is not all that easy, but a rule of thumb that will enable us to get clear about it is to say that if you are doing more than 50% of the work in the interview it isn't counseling. Producing brilliant and subtle interpretations is not counseling, no matter how profound and insightful they are. Nor does couching the interpretations in esoteric or psychological language make them counseling.

An activity becomes counseling when it has the character of a joint process of discovery, with the astrologer and client operating in more or less equal partnership.

The purpose of counseling can be defined as leading the client to see that he does not have to go on repeating the same old patterns—however powerful these patterns may seem to be.

Pehaps the most **basic rule** of any kind of counseling, and from which the other rules more or less automatically derive, is *Give up your need to be right*. Without exception, *all* counselors, therapists and dealers in specialist information have a tremendous emotional investment in their own particular theory or discipline. This is true whether it is astrology, psychoanalysis, tarot, Jungian analysis, TA, Gestalt, or whatever. It is, indeed, inevitable. Unless a particular discipline held a deeply satisfying emotional charge for the practitioner, he or she would scarcely have been sufficiently motivated to become proficient in it. The attraction to and choice to work in any particular field will, like anything else, have a great deal of script energy in it. So the practitioner will feel irrationally threatened if his system is challenged.

I think that perhaps astrologers are especially vulnerable to feeling threatened in such a way. For a start, the discipline itself does not have any establishment authority behind it. Compare the astrologer's case with that of a doctor, for example. Medicine carries a huge weight of authority simply because of its acceptance by the state and the amount of funding and research that goes into it. Individual doctors have gone through periods of lengthy and rigorous training and their qualifications are legally recognized. An individual medical practitioner might have worries about his own competence to apply his training—and his patients might worry about it too—but there is pretty well 100% agreement for the validity of medicine as a system of healing. Whatever kind of credit to his profession he might personally be, no doctor has to worry about proving that medicine works.

In contrast, the astrologer, especially the inexperienced one, not only has to worry about his own personal competence but about whether his discipline is valid. There is a good chance that any given client is likely to be at least a little skeptical about astrology, so the astrologer is on the defensive right from the start. Worse than that, the astrologer's own conviction of the validity of astrology is quite likely to be shaky. It is not a university subject, it is supported by practically no funding or research and no one in any kind of established authority takes it seriously—or not publicly, at any rate. What research has been done seems, at best, to show that there is *some* validity in it. For example, the best known work, that of Michel Gauquelin, indicates merely that the planets, when emphasized by angular position, do correspond with an emphasis in the character on much the kind of traits that one would expect from astrological tradition. Gauquelin's findings hardly support astrological practice as a whole and, indeed, he himself goes out of his way to insist that they do not. As far as I am aware at the moment of writing, no research has so far shown up any evidence at all for the validity of signs as they are normally used.

As for houses, there is little agreement even within the tradition, let alone support from research—though, as noted, Gauquelin's work gives some support to the notion of the importance of planets on angles.

And worse than all this, most astrologers have had the experience of giving information based on specific chart factors, which was seemingly accurate, and then finding that the chart was wrong. This is enough to shake anyone's faith. By some variant of Murphy's Law (If anything can go wrong, it will), it usually happens with a client whom one especially wanted to impress with the rigorous, scientific nature of astrology.

All of these difficulties can be handled easier if one can accept that astrology is not a rational, scientific subject susceptible to statistical research. It is, in essence, profoundly nonrational and paradoxical. Of course, there is a side to it that looks rational. The fact that, given accurate data, a chart can be calculated very precisely and that all sorts of sophisticated mathematical operations can be performed on the basic chart which yield further information certainly gives it the appearance of being on a par with a subject like, say, economics. Again, the fact that chart factors have more or less standardized and agreed-upon meanings that can be put together, even by a computer, to give a recognizably accurate portrait of a person makes it look as though it were a cut and dried, logical discipline. As remarked earlier, many astrologers seem to take the view that, if we only had more data, we would *really* know how astrology works. On this view, it looks as though astrology were at present in a state analogous to that of medicine in the nineteenth century. At that time all the major discoveries that make modern medicine what it is were still to be made. Seemingly, we still have to discover the astrological equivalent of microbes and anesthetics. If this analogy were valid, it would certainly seem that research is the answer, and that to get astrology accepted in the way that allopathic medicine is accepted, we simply need more basic information.

But the analogy is not valid. The scientific disciplines operate on a system of clearly defined cause and effect. They became more efficient and powerful as research established the chains of cause and effect. Moreover, scientific disciplines have as their basic philosophical assumption the Cartesian postulate that man is separate from the universe.

Astrology, on the other hand, is demonstrably not a cause and effect system. So far as I am aware, the only person of any standing who has recognized this and attempted to handle it is Jung, with his theory of synchronicity. The theory seems to lack much impact mainly, I think, because Jung, having acknowledged the existence of an "acausal connecting principle" then proceeds to discuss it in a way that makes it look like a more subtle variant of causality. Our entire language and thought structure depend on causality. It is quite impossible to capture and define an acausal principle in causal language. It makes no sense to do it and it doesn't work. It is like trying to define poetry by mathematical formulae. All we can really do is to accept that there are some areas of life that cannot usefully be examined through the spectacles of causality. It helps to do this if we look at causality as a convenient framework, or set of rules, that enables us to handle many aspects of the material world. What gets in the way so badly when we try to examine subjects like astrology is that we have elevated causality to the level of an immutable fact of the universe against which everything else has to be measured.

Cause and effect seems mainly to be a property of the universe when it is viewed in the framework of objectivity. In other words, when we come from the Cartesian context of man's separateness from the universe, we need to postulate, or to create, causality in order to have the system work. Astrology, however, comes from the context that man and the universe are a single, indivisible entity. Within this context, *we do not need to create causality in order to have the system work.* It's as simple as that and the whole debate about the scientific basis of astrology is a gigantic red herring. I find it amazing that anyone could imagine that computer studies based on the assumption of an objective universe separate from consciousness could discover anything useful about astrology which is based on exactly the opposite assumption. The fact that some computer studies produce results that correspond with what you would get from astrology is not so much evidence of the value of computer studies as an indication that the basic truth in astrology is so powerful that it will manifest through *any* kind of distorting filter.

This may seem like a digression from the issue of counseling and the purpose of this chapter. But these are issues that will come up for the astrologer and get in the way of giving up the need to be right. If you are run by a more or less unconscious need to justify and prove astrology you will have a tendency to insist upon your interpretations and to force them upon the client. Some astrologers habitually begin an interview by impressing the client and getting one up on him by a recital of chart interpretation. If they score enough accurate hits, the client is stunned into acquiescence in the validity of astrology and the competence of the practitioner. It's a fair enough strategy for some types of work, but it isn't a counseling approach.

We live in a world which operates on causality, and astrology does not conform to that world. To do effective counseling, we need to acknowledge that, to acknowledge all the fears and doubts and defensiveness that come up around it and simply allow them to be there. Eventually they will move to destruction like anything else that is simply allowed to be. They simply cease to be an issue. Every once in a while, they will get reactivated by a client who behaves in a challenging manner or by a hostile magazine article about astrology. Just allow whatever is there to be there. If you argue about it, defend yourself or fret over it, it will gain mass and persist.

None of this is easy to do. The monkey mind wants to be right; it cannot conceive of getting beyond the issues of right and wrong. Nevertheless, this is what has to be done. It amounts to conducting the interview by being willing to come from your Real Self, which is surely likely to be a better guide than a drunk, obsessed, angry monkey!

Obviously, we all go through a phase where we need to discover for ourselves that astrology does work. To do counseling one needs to be at a point where one's own interpretational skills are not an issue. But astrology is no different from anything else in this respect. A doctor or a plumber needs to be skilled enough not to have to have the bulk of his attention on figuring out what to do next. This is why, even for an experienced and skilled astrologer, I am now in favor of having fairly full written notes to work from or, at least, a written list of the basic chart themes. Wrestling with a client's mind is tricky and demanding enough without having to wonder whether you know what you're really doing.

Rule 2 is *Always be where the client is*. This means no moralizing and no judgments. If moralizing and judgments come up, as they will from time to time, then acknowledge them and allow them to be there. It is a matter of totally acknowledging and accepting what the client currently perceives as his reality. Sometimes what happens is that the client reveals a system of values that clashes with your own and reactivates your script patterns so that you feel discomfited and even threatened. For example, you may feel turned off by what the client says about his sexual preferences. Or, for that matter, you may be turned on by it. Either reaction needs to be acknowledged and allowed to be there so that it can process out and not get in the way of the session. When I say acknowledged, I mean inwardly. It may sometimes be appropriate to share a positive reaction with a client. Rarely, if ever, is it appropriate to share a negative one because it will be perceived as rejection. Occasionally something comes up which won't process out and leaves you in a state of emotional charge after the session. In this case, clear it up by sharing it with a friend afterward or work on it with a therapist. Don't burden the client with it.

Sometimes what happens is that you can see the client obviously avoiding a major issue. If he talks about how wonderful his relationships are and you can see a juicy Venus-Neptune aspect in the chart, it can be very tempting to want to say, "Oh, come off it. Stop kidding yourself!" It is not that such an intervention is inherently wrong. It is that, if it is going to be made, it needs to be made appropriately and when it will have a constructive effect. A good degree of rapport and communication is obviously necessary in order to enable you to judge when to intervene in such a way. The important thing is to accept the client's level of reality as being a valid "what's so" for him. If you validate where he is at, he will begin to move off it automatically. It is as though, by offering no resistance to what he says, you create a space for it to be dissipated. A seeming exception to this rule is when the client exhibits resistance by getting into the superficial detail. In this case, to get anywhere, you have to keep confronting him to get at what it means to him, what his thoughts and feelings are. However, you can still do this from a position of acceptance; you don't have to make him wrong for doing it, irritating though it may be.

This is a good point at which to draw the distinction between sympathy and compassion. Etymologically, they both mean the same—"feeling with"—but in practice they are quite different. Compassion is what I'm talking about—a nonjudgmental acceptance of everything about the other person. You don't have to like it or agree with it. In fact, you may have the very strong view that the person needs to clear up whatever it is as fast as possible.

For example, a client might tell you that she hates her husband, and you may feel that the hatred is very unpleasant and ugly and that holding on to it is what keeps her stuck in an unhappy marriage. And you may well be right, but it will do no good to tell her so until you have established the right conditions of compassion and acceptance. Equally, agreeing with her that he is a monster and that her feelings are justified will effectively block any possibility of her moving through the hatred and transforming it.

Implicit in compassion is the recognition that the other person has the strength and resources to handle her difficulties. It is a condition in which you are not being sucked into agreement with or rejection of the other person's drama but being accepting of it as the material that is up to be worked with. It is essentially a recognition of the person's Real Self.

Sympathy, on the other hand, is essentially going into agreement with the other person's drama and taking the struggles of the monkey too seriously. There is always an implied "poor you" in it and the assumption that her difficulties are bigger than she is. It is virtually never appropriate in counseling—not the type of counseling that we are discussing, anyway. This does not mean that you should ride roughshod over a client's feelings. It means accepting the reality of the hatred or distress or despair or whatever it is, while at the same time recognizing the existence of a frame of reference in which the negative feelings do not have an ultimate reality and do not have to be taken so seriously.

Indeed, sometimes a client may have become so desensitized to serious deprivation that it is necessary to point out to him that the circumstances of his life really are terrible. People can get so fixated on a very low level of fulfillment that it is almost impossible for them to imagine a more expansive way of life. It may well be appropriate to have them look at how awful things are, but without your going into agreement with it and becoming emotionally involved. It is necessary to keep your own sense of levels of reality clear and not to lose sight of the higher frame of reference.

It is impossible to cover every eventuality and to prescribe a way of handling it, and to try to do so would make counseling sound far more complicated and difficult than it really is. If you are truly willing to let your client be the way he is, and not the way you think he should be, and it is truly your purpose to empower him to enhance the quality of his life, you will intuitively know what to do. And you will only know when you do it. It is not possible to do this kind of work by the book. In a sense, the only rule is that there are no rules *and* the rules I am suggesting will give you a basic format within which you can work.

Rule 3 is simply *Listen*. This means not only listening to the words but also the attitudes and feelings behind the words. It also means observing the body language that your client uses. It means putting all your own reactions on hold (not suppressing them). For astrologers, it especially means not impatiently waiting for the client to finish so that you can burst in with a wonderful piece of interpretation from the chart.

It amounts to hearing what your client is communicating so that you recreate what he or she is experiencing within yourself. Always ask the client what he is experiencing. Never assume that you know. People may have very different experiences of very similar events. The death of a parent, for example, may mean terrible grief for one person and relief for another.

It is not uncommon for people in our culture to be so out of touch with feelings that they confuse them with opinions. If you say to someone, "How did you feel when your mother died?" he may say something like, "I felt all the arrangements went very well." It may take considerable persistence to get at the actual feelings that are present.

I do not, on the whole, encourage the dramatic expression of feelings during the session since this can get in the way of moving through the feelings. Sometimes feelings burst in upon a person in an irresistible way and then it is best to allow them to move to completion. If a client bursts into tears, I offer Kleenex and wait until it is over. When such feelings have started to be expressed, at that point I usually encourage the client to go on with them.

Explosions of feelings are not always negative. I had one client who became so exuberant about a piece of insight that I had some difficulty in calming her down and getting her to see that the job wasn't done simply because she had hit a layer of good feelings.

Always be where the client is at. Validate the expression of feeling if it occurs, but don't let the client get stuck in it.

An exception to my general rule of not particularly seeking to provoke the expression of feelings is that I always encourage laughter. Laughter is a healing mechanism in itself and usually results when the client gets into the higher frame of reference and sees the absurdity of what his obsessed survival mechanism is up to. This, of course, is to be distinguished from laughing at oneself as a defense mechanism, which is a way of pretending that the painful feelings are not there. With the healing laughter, one is fully validating the painfulness of the feelings but refusing to take them so seriously for the moment, refusing to get enmeshed in the drama and importance of them. It is as though the actor playing Hamlet were suddenly to see that he has been agonizing over Ophelia's death for real.

Sometimes a sharp and clear reflecting back to the client of what is actually going on will provoke this healing laughter. With one client— who had a strong Virgo-Capricorn emphasis—we identified a deep-rooted belief that basically she didn't count, that whatever she did had no real effect on others. I tried to get her to look at this belief from the point of view of it being there by her own choice and intention. She began to get angry with me and accused me of pushing her, not giving her space and not paying enough attention to her feelings.

I was rather slow to see that this was a manifestation of the basic context of not counting. The intensity of her anger reactivated me and I became defensive. I started to justify my actions and to try to accommodate her objections. After a couple of minutes or so, and just when I thought I was losing control of the session, I saw what was happening. As if the subject had not been mentioned before, I remarked, "Oh, I think I see what's going on. You're feeling like you don't count!"

This immediately provoked laughter as she perceived the obsessiveness with which her survival mechanism was continuing to pursue something which, at another level, she had already recognized as being merely a belief. In a case like this, the laughter seems to come spontaneously from the acceptance of and taking responsibility for the pattern. The French philosopher Henri Bergson said that humor arises from seeing a living thing behaving in a mechanical and predictable way. This is the sort of laughter that arises when we catch ourselves in mechanical behavior, and especially when we see how much emotional energy we are investing in it. Of course, one should never laugh *at* the client. That would be completely invalidating, and I would hardly have thought it necessary to mention except that it once happened to me, when I was on the receiving end of a session.

The incident with the lady who thought she didn't count is also a good example of the fact that there is no particular right way to do it. Every counseling session is unique and develops out of the interaction between yourself and your client. If your intentions are clear then the session will work, and whatever happens, including mistakes, will be useful material.

Implicit in the rule of total listening is being conscious all the time of what is going on in yourself. What happened in that encounter was that I got stuck on being right about what I was doing and started to push my client a little too soon toward taking a detached attitude to her belief that she didn't count. If I had not been able to let go of my need to be right I would not have perceived what was happening clearly enough to be able to turn it to advantage instead of letting it wreck the encounter.

Really, all you have to do and, ultimately, all you *can* do is to get out of the client's way so that his own natural healing process can take place. Ideally, you serve as a perfect mirror for him, assisting him consciously to recreate the patterns that he originally created unconsciously.

As I hinted in the last chapter, you sometimes get clients whose secret intention is that the session shall be a failure. In TA terms, they are people whose Adapted Child is stuck on a position that nobody can help them and that nobody is any good anyway. If it were just that, you would never see them because they wouldn't go near an astrologer or a therapist in the first place—what would be the point? But, in these cases, the Adapted Child also has a compulsion to prove how right it is to be on that position every once in a while. So, you will get a person who may not be openly skeptical—may, indeed, be cooperative and eager—yet who is inwardly determined to sabotage the session.

I haven't seen enough of this phenomenon to be certain of spotting it from the chart. A factor that puts me on the alert for it, though, is a hard aspect between Moon and Pluto, including the quincunx. To a lesser extent, I am wary of a hard aspect between Mercury and Pluto, though these people are more likely to be candid about their skepticism. They may be—and usually are—very resistant and difficult to work with but the intention to sabotage is either overt or lightly disguised. I am not saying that every client with these aspects will be a secret saboteur, but they are a common factor in the charts of clients I have seen who have had some degree or other of this quality. A hard aspect of Moon to Saturn does not, of itself, seem to indicate the saboteur, but if it is present in addition to a hard Moon-Pluto, it does seem to reinforce the tendency.

In any case, the trick is to spot it and confront it before the client can throw the switch. Sometimes a client will start off by telling you that he has been in analysis for three years, has had his chart done a couple of times already and has been to heaven knows how many groups and therapy sessions, and none of it has done the slightest bit of good. He may regale you with the shortcomings of his analyst and the other astrologers he has seen. And all this with a sad, sweet smile that says, "But, of course, I can tell *you* this because I know *you're* different."

It will be done much more subtly than this, of course, and it can be very plausible and seductive stuff, especially in one's early days of counseling when one hasn't much experience and feels insecure about it. However, that sad, sweet smile will lure you onto the point of a bayonet if you fall for it. The best thing to do is to say, as neutrally and nonjudgmentally as possible, "It looks to me as though you may have a pattern of setting it up so that you prove that no one can do anything for you so you wind up disappointed and maybe secretly triumphant." Depending on how confronting you want to be, you can then add, "Are you intending to do that with me?" The thing is to treat it exactly as you would treat any other pattern that comes up; it's neither good nor bad but simply material to be worked with.

If the client admits to the pattern, you can then proceed to explore it. If he denies it, you can say, "I still think it's a possibility we ought to look at," and ask him what his feelings are when he realizes that he has got nothing out of his other sessions. (In fact, a good general rule is, *When in doubt, ask for a feeling.*) But, whatever happens, don't get attached to winning with this person. If your stratagem is successful it is easy to get charged up on the notion that you really are the first one who is going to be smart enough to crack this tough nut. Then you have jumped into the trap that was set for you even after you have recognized it.

But, unfortunately, not all the saboteurs will signal their intentions in this way, or at all. With this type of client it is almost as though he wants to be found out and perhaps to be reassured that you are not such an idiot as to fall for his tricks. A small percentage of clients play a much harder and trickier game. They go along with whatever you do and you really feel that you are getting through to them and making progress. Then, at a critical moment, perhaps near the end of the session, they do something that completely rejects and invalidates everything that has happened. It is pretty much game, set and match to the client at that point. You can try to salvage something from the wreckage, but the fact is that you have been conned. About all you can do is to see your client to the door as graciously as possible and then examine yourself to see what went wrong and what you were so anxious to be right about that allowed your client to hook you.

Unpleasant and humiliating as these encounters are, they need to be treated as valuable learning experiences. Which is to say that they need to be looked at nonjudgmentally and in a context of being responsible for creating them. They are thrown up from time to time by your own psyche because you are stuck on something that you need to move off.

This kind of encounter with clients can be illuminated by the Transactional Analysis theory of "games." A game is a series of plausible transactions that actually are moving to an ulterior payoff. The person playing the game gets to experience a favorite bad feeling. The *intention* to experience the bad feeling is unconscious. The payoff of the game is to prove how right one is to have a certain position about life. As I have suggested, the clients who secretly intend to sabotage the session probably play games that have the payoff of proving that nobody is any good. Games cannot be played without a partner, so if a client has successfully played a game and got his payoff, then you too have played a complementary game and got your payoff.

It is, I suggest, less useful to concern yourself about analyzing the games your clients may be playing than to get clear about the game that you are playing. If you stop playing your side of it, the clients will have no opportunity to play theirs. The games played by the astrologer in these circumstances will usually be variants of what Eric Berne called "Kick Me."

What it amounts to is that your monkey mind has the notion that a certain amount of feeling helpless, clumsy and humiliated is necessary for your survival. So, every so often, you unconsciously initiate, or get hooked into, behavior that proves just how right that is. Don't make a conscious effort to stop it; that's only resisting it and making it persist. Allow it to be there and to process out. You will know when it has cleared up by the fact that your clients no longer play sabotage games—or no longer play them successfully.

Counseling is a continuous learning process, more so than interpretation is. It is true that you can always learn more about what astrological symbols mean, but there comes a time when your store of information on the subject is large enough so that the acquisition of more becomes more a matter of polishing and fine-tuning than radical improvement. To some degree, the same can be said of counseling *technique*. You can acquire a level of skill in handling an interview that becomes more or less automatic. But, as I said at the beginning of the chapter, counseling is a joint process of discovery. It is not only your client's psyche that has a spotlight on it but your own as well. At the end of the session, you should not only have empowered the client to enhance the quality of his life but also empowered yourself to enhance the quality of yours. If you haven't got something for yourself out of it other than your fee, it has been information giving and not counseling.

This method for using the astrological chart is at a very early stage and we are all still beginners. Everything that I have said and the examples I will be giving later are meant to be taken as guidelines for discovering your own approach to effective astrological counseling rather than as hard and fast rules to be mechanically applied.

9

Client Interviews

The following dialogues are transcripts of tapes of actual sessions, used by permission of the people concerned. Names have been changed and such personal details as might give a clue to identity omitted, but otherwise the charts are correct and the transcripts only lightly edited. They are, inevitably, somewhat repetitious. One of the salient features of this work is the need to constantly bring the client back to the issue in its plainest terms. The resistance put up by the mind is very evident in these scripts.

What will be unfamiliar to the astrological reader and, perhaps, at first sight disconcerting, is the use that I make of the information from the chart. The astrologer who is accustomed to dwelling at length on individual features of the chart and giving a lot of detailed information may feel that I am reducing the importance of the astrology. This is not so. The difference between this way of working and the more conventional type of astrological interview is that I use the chart information with the intention of getting a result and not as an end in itself. The result aimed for is that the client have a clear and unambiguous confrontation with one or more of the major unconscious organizing principles of his or her life. To this end, it seems to me more effective to present the information in terms of the broad themes of the chart, which are selected to include all the significant details. As mentioned in Chapter 7, once the confrontation has taken place and has been clearly established, I will often spend some time giving detailed information. However, I regard this as optional and I have not included any examples of it as it would increase the length of the dialogues to no real purpose, and it differs very little from the conventional information-giving interview.

I want to stress again the point made in the first chapter that the purpose of the interview is not understanding but, for want of a better word, "enlightenment." And what I mean by "enlightenment" in this context is an experiential grasp of a major operating principle of the life. For me, the giving of information is essentially an input of energy. It is intended to light up the relevant psychological circuits so that we can see what is actually so about them. In much the same way, an electrician will put a potential across an electrical circuit to check out how it is working. Giving information in broad terms lights up more circuits and gets the interview off to a faster start.

So, I want to be clear that the chart itself plays a different part in this method from the one that it plays in the conventional astrological session. At first sight, it may appear to be a lesser one. One could conduct this sort of interview with information gained from any source and it is certainly not specific to astrology. One could equally well use information gained from conventional psychological tests, the client's dreams or fantasies, tarot, numerology, palmistry or clairvoyant perception. To repeat, the essence of this counseling method lies in the *use* of the information, not in the derivation of it.

I would, however, argue that the astrological chart is far and away the best source of information. The meanings of the astrological symbols are generally well understood and, for the most part, generally agreed upon. The meanings of the planets in signs, houses and by aspects has been checked out in clinical practice often enough to establish basic standard meanings. As I have argued in Chapter 5, although a given factor, such as Venus in Gemini, will not manifest in exactly the same way in two different people, there is nevertheless a common basic meaning that will be applicable in all cases and can be used as a starting point. Chart interpretation can be very reliable and does not have to depend on any special psychic or clairvoyant gifts—which too often seem to be affected by factors outside the person's control. The interpretation can be prepared ahead of time so that you can have your full attention on the client. Finally, the quantity and range of information available from the chart is unparalled and the level of it can be readily adjusted to the needs of the individual client.

As will be evident from the dialogues, I am not so much concerned with analysis as such as I am with having the client confront the obvious. Analysis leads, or can lead, to more and more understanding. The client has more and more reasons for being the way he is. This kind of head knowledge has no power to make a difference. Jung refers somewhere to a young man who produced a full written self-analysis of his neurosis, as perceptive and accurate as Jung could have done himself. And it made no difference because it remained at the stage of head knowledge and, as such, not really confronted in the young man's experience.

Analysis is a blind alley as long as it is used for looking for reasons and causes in the past. It does have a value in that it can enable the person to get a clearer grasp of what's so NOW. Clients do talk about childhood experiences and their relationships with their parents and I encourage this as part of seeing what is so for them in the present. As I have remarked in Chapter 3, the parent-child drama is the life drama played out in a starker and simpler form, and the issues are not covered up and obscured in the way in which they are in later life. In two of the dialogues the clients spend a lot of time looking at childhood issues. It is not, to my way of looking at it now, that the childhood issues contain any magic key to the situation. It is rather that whatever the client comes up with as being an issue in childhood is also the issue now. I don't usually initiate talking about parents, but sometimes, if the client seems to be going round and round on the surface of things, I will do so.

Many clients, especially if they have done some thinking about themselves and perhaps had some therapy, are often in the position of someone who has all the pieces of a jigsaw puzzle and has even assembled them correctly but who still doesn't recognize the picture he is looking at. What I aim to do in this case is the equivalent of having the client look at the picture he has and tell him, "What you've got there is a picture of a rhinoceros." He can't *see* that it's a picture of a rhinoceros because he is too busy trying to figure out the deeper significance of the horn and the tail and wondering why the creature should have four legs.

Again, to repeat what I have said earlier, seeing and confronting the obvious requires a condition of a kind of childlike naivete, the ability to see something for what it *is*, as distinct from one's judgments and expectations about it. Another reason people can't see that they have a picture of a rhinoceros is that, after they had put together two or three pieces of a gray colored animal, they just *knew* it had to be an elephant. Or, maybe all along what they really wanted was a lion.

This comes out very strongly in the first dialogue with Martin, where he is so focused on what he believes to be a need to get more in touch with feelings about his mother, who died when he was seven, that he can't see that what he actually needs to be handling is his *inability* to get in touch with his feelings about her.

Unfortunately, the dialogues cannot really convey the feeling and atmosphere of the session and, in cold black and white, it may sometimes look as though I am being flippant or unsympathetic. I always aim to come from the assumption that the client is bigger than his problems and I attempt to set that tone right from the beginning of the session. That can sometimes mean that I will say things like "OK, so you want to kill your husband. So what?" It can look callous but it is an attempt to jolt the client into looking at whatever it is from the higher perspective. It is not an invalidation of some awful thing that the client has come out with but an acceptance of it. I don't do it unless I feel that the level of communication between myself and the client is good enough for such an intervention to be appropriate and for it to be correctly perceived by the client.

The sessions always begin with a preliminary discussion, lasting about twenty minutes, on the basic framework that we are going to use. The notions of choosing our lives, the survival-oriented mind that obscures the obvious issues, the need to confront and take responsibility for these issues so that they can process out through the natural create-maintain-destroy cycle are all discussed. I always present the analogy of the survival-oriented mind as the monkey caught with his paw in the gourd, and frequently refer to "the monkey" later to call attention to what the client's mind is up to. I explain that the session proper will largely be about handling the resistance of the mind to confronting the obvious. I specifically state that I don't want him to *believe* any of this but to be willing to adopt it as ground rules of the game that we are going to be playing for the next hour and a half or couple of hours.

I always have in mind that the session will last an hour and a half but I am prepared for it to last longer, and I never book another client or any other activity close to the expected end of the session. I always have the target that the client is going to have his life completely turned around in one session. As far as I know, this has never actually happened, but it is a wonderful way of focusing your own intention and follows the lead of Eric Berne, the creator of Transactional Analysis.

The session proper then begins with me reading out the first of my list of the chart themes and asking for a reaction to it. Though, as I remarked earlier, this way of working may look as though it diminishes the importance of the chart, in practice it is far from being so. The greater your understanding of astrology and the more thorough and detailed your preliminary analysis of the chart, the more likely you are to be able to condense it into broad statements that will really strike home and light up the client's circuits in a useful way.

MARTIN: Major Chart Themes

1. Something of a compulsive achiever. Places a lot of value on having control, both over himself and others. Strong sense of self-discipline,

duty, responsibility. Does not allow himself much pleasure. Can be a genuinely charismatic, inspiring leader.

2.   His sense of what is expected of him in the world is very confused—even totally divided against himself. Probably highly inconsistent and unpredictable behavior from parents. Feels misunderstood and reacts by being provocative and challenging. Tends to create a good many crises, partly out of a desire for drama and sensation, partly in order to find out what makes other people tick.

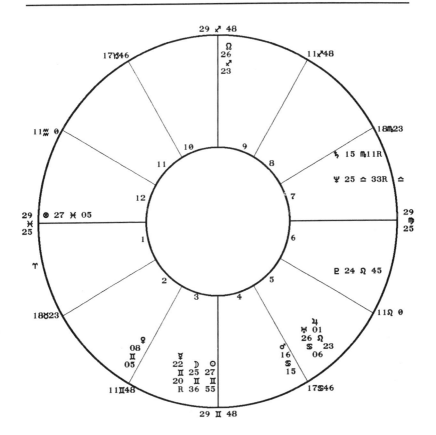

Figure 1.9.1 Martin. Born June 20, 1955 at 1:15 A.M., B.S.T., in Chesterfield England. Topocentric houses used for calculations. This data comes from his mother's recollection of his birth. Calculations by Astro-Computing Services.

3. Impressionable, hypersensitive, easily feels threatened or intruded upon. Tendency to lethargy, to withdraw into inner world, inclined to be passive and resigned. A lot of energy is focused on the past in some way—may be bitter feelings about something, perhaps inadequate mother love.

4. Strong sexual nature, central to entire life, but creates many difficulties about it. A basic capacity for open, warm, natural and harmonious flow of love and sex yet distrusts free flow of feelings. May feel that relationships are so highly emotionally charged that they are potentially destructive and best avoided altogether.

5. His basic expectations of others tend to be rather fixed and somewhat unrealistic, therefore he is vulnerable to a good deal of disappointment. Particularly tends to idealize women. At the same time, he needs a large circle of friends and the support of like-minded others for emotional balance and sexual functioning.

Martin is 26 years old and an accountant. I have left out the preliminary discussion and the information-giving at the end. Otherwise, this is an almost complete transcript of the session. I have made comments in parentheses where it seems necessary. Readers need to imagine frequent encouraging noises, "yeses" and "uh-uhs" from me which would have added to the physical length of the transcript without contributing to the substance of it. Throughout the transcripts, I am indicated as "R" and the client by the appropriate initial.

R: We'll start off by looking at the major themes of the chart and see what kind of bells they ring. Okay, first one. "Something of a compulsive achiever. Places a lot of value on having control, both over himself and others. Strong sense of self-discipline, duty, responsibility. Does not allow himself much pleasure. Can be a genuinely charismatic, inspiring leader." Any reactions to that?

M: That is one part of me but there is another part, almost the opposite. Sometimes the compulsiveness gets very strong indeed. Most things I do I do compulsively.

R: What about having control? Controlling and being in a dominant position seem to be important areas in your life.

M: Yes, I do seem to set it up that way. For example, I work for myself so I have control. I am worried about control. It's a position I always seem to get myself into. When I was a child, I often wondered why I had to make myself so important.

(So far, so good. There's no strong reaction here. The interaction has gone some way to creating confidence in the validity of the chart but there is nothing to really get hold of. The issue of control will become important later on but for now there is nothing to be gained by dwelling on this first point.)

R: Right, let's move on to point two. "His sense of what is expected of him in the world is very confused—even totally divided against himself. Probably highly inconsistent and unpredictable behavior from parents. Feels misunderstood and reacts by being provocative and challenging. Tends to create a good many crises, partly out of the desire for drama and sensation, partly in order to find out what makes other people tick."

M: I have had a good many crises and it's true there's a part of me that wants a sense of drama out of life. It *is* difficult for me to know what's expected of me. As you say, I'm divided against myself and terribly confused. My mother died when I was seven years old and it's my relationship with her that I can't get sorted out. It feels alive with something or other, some very highly charged emotion that I can't put my finger on. There's something very deeply locked in my subconscious. I feel that I was terribly involved with her and that part of me I can't get access to.

(Definitely something to go for here. This piece of information has really lit up one of his circuits, so we start off by finding out more about it.)

R: What are you doing about it? What's your attitude to that part you can't get access to?

M: I almost can't believe I have it; that's a major problem. I don't have many specific memories, which is causing me a lot of problems. I get quite disheartened by it at times. I've been doing some therapy and trying to work my way through it but I seem to be thrashing in the dark.

R: Do you have a belief that goes, "I can't get on with my life until I've dug into this stuff about my mother?" (Reflect back what they are saying in as plain and cogent a way as you can.)

M: Yes.

(This is it! We've hit the major issue about ten minutes into the session proper. The thing now is to push hard to get more clarity on and acceptance of this belief system. It is a severe vicious circle. He can't get on with his life until he's sorted out the stuff with his mother, and he can't do that so he can't get on with his life.)

R: Well, that's it. This is exactly what I was talking about in the abstract. This is a nut that your monkey mind has got hold of. There's some pattern there that goes, "I don't really make it with my mother and I don't know what it's all about and this is the way my life is. In order to survive I have to struggle and fret about it and on top of that I'm scared of it too because I don't know what will come up."

The way you're going to get through that is to kind of put the whole thing up on a screen and just observe that what's so for you is that you have all this stuff that you think you can't get at and you think must be there. And also be aware of the feelings and value judgments that you have around it. They'll prevent you from just simply seeing what's there if you get stuck in them so you have to become aware of them too. What are some of the things that come up around it?

M: I have a sense of being tormented by my mother and looked at in a very sexual way by her. And I feel a lot of anger towards her, as though I'm guarding myself. There also seems to be a lot of guilt about not being able to get these memories back.

R: Are you willing to have all that stuff just be there, just be what it is.

M: Well, I know it's all there. (Rather puzzled; he's not really getting it yet.)

R: What happens when you do that; look at it all impersonally?

(Keep things moving. Have the client work.)

M: (long pause) The immediate thing that comes to me is that I shouldn't push it so hard. Because I push very hard. It's in my nature.

R: Remember the create-maintain-destroy cycle. You created *all* that stuff and you're maintaining it. And one of the ways you go on maintaining it is through the feeling that you have to push at it and dig into it. If you can just let it be it will move.

M: I'm aware of a part of me that wants to maintain this drama. I can feel that very much.

(He still isn't really "getting" it. There is intellectual agreement with what I am saying but little or no experience.)

M: (apparently at a tangent to what he has just said) I'm aware of a strong side of me that wants to meet someone and settle down. If that happens, I *will* leave all this behind. But there's a whole drama around my mother's death and my father's remarriage that I'm locked into. I haven't yet been able to get on my own two feet and leave that behind me and get on with my own life. It's starting to happen but it's taking a long time.

R: When we look at these things *clearly* they get destroyed and that happens somehow outside of space and time. So, I want to get your attention off the process of it that does take time. Look, this may sound fanciful, but there is a Buddhist sect that says that the universe is created and destroyed forty thousand times a second—which, as a matter of fact, fits in with what we know from particle physics. Maybe, when you really see something clearly, you destroy your universe as it is, for an inconceivable fraction of a second. Then you create it again but something's missing. The block has gone—at one level, the level of creation, though you still have to go through a process about it.

There's a big vicious circle in what you said a minute ago about wanting to find somebody to settle down with and *when* you do that you'll be able to clear up the stuff with your mother. There's a big "if only" in that. In fact you can do it NOW. In terms of looking at it from this purely objective view you can get beyond all the stuff about your mother's death and your father's remarriage.

M: (long sigh as if confronted with enormous task) Well!!! Could I? Could I? (in a tone of doubt and skepticism)

R: You just did, at least partly. (A reference to M saying earlier that he knew it was all there. It wasn't a big experience but he got enough sense of his Real Self to get a message that pushing hard at his stuff wouldn't work. Reinforce and encourage even tiny breakthroughs.)

M: There have been other times recently when I've also felt that. Just for a brief instant, I could see my way through all this.

R: Yes. What happens is that, for a fraction of a second, you get to see that you are you and not the monkey who's struggling with the nuts. Then the monkey tries twice as hard to hold on to them because he needs them to survive—or so he thinks.

M: I'm beginning to start feeling like a protesting child who's saying, "No, I won't play with the world." That's often the way I feel.

R: Well, don't beat yourself up for it and don't get stuck in feeling proud of it either. Just notice that it's there. "Oh, look, I've got this withdrawal thing and I don't want to play with the world." Once you can start to withdraw the sense of it being a big deal then you unblock the natural flow.

What I want you to do when you go out of here is to start looking at your life as though it were one of those simulated driving trainers. *Whatever* comes up on the screen is what you need to look at and acknowledge and handle. What gets in the way of doing this is that the things that come up look so obvious or trivial or overwhelming that we think, "This can't be it. What I'm really after is down the next street on the left." So we never get any further because the dog running across the road goes on running across the road until we deal with it instead of having our attention on what we think is the *real* issue around the next corner. The problem with it is that we all find it so hard to recognize the obvious.

M: For me, at the moment, I feel like I've heard what you've said but it's all starting to swirl round a bit. I'm struggling with what you're saying. I'm glad I've got the tape to go back and listen to.

(Yes, but don't rely on the tape. He might lose it or have it break down. Get him clear now if at all possible.)

R: What are you struggling with? What's not clear about it?

M: Well, I *hear* what you say then I wonder if I'll remember it. I wonder if I'll take note of it. I'm afraid I'm going to push it to one side and carry on exactly as before.

R: That sounds like a good typical piece of monkey mind.

(Put the fear that he won't get it into context. It is just another belief about the issue. I might perhaps have elaborated a little more here, though Martin breaks in very quickly with his next remark.)

M: And what you're saying is reminding me of what I've read in Carlos Castaneda. Don Juan talks about looking for the obvious. I have a very highly developed intellect and I'm very good at solving impossible problems. Ask me to do something obvious and I'll get into a terrible knot and lose my temper.

R: To bring it back to concrete terms, the obvious thing for you at the moment is that you have this stuff about your mother *and you cannot get to it*. And that's it! That's the dog running across the road. You have it and you can't get to it and you feel guilty about it and if only you met the right woman...all that stuff, that's what's obvious about you. What you're doing with it is what you've just been saying—to try to get into the nearly impossible part that you don't really remember and not dealing with what's actually there. It sounds stupid to put it this way but, really, life boils down to the simple proposition that what is, is and what isn't, isn't. We spend so much time trying to handle what isn't there but we think should be that we never handle what is there. And then we wonder why we don't get anywhere!

M: That reminds me instantly that, often, especially in the therapy I've been doing, that I'm looking to see what they're driving at. I'm looking for some terrible dark secret. My mind is capable of generating enormous things out of very little...I just wanted to tell you that; it rang bells with me.

R: Okay, are you doing that now?

(Obviously a crucial point; we'll never get anywhere if he *is* doing it now.)

M: No, not at the moment. I'm very engaged at the moment.

(Meaning he is fully present and focused on what's going on; his expression and body language confirm his words.)

R: Let's move on to point three, then. "Impressionable, hypersensitive, easily feels threatened or intruded upon. Tendency to lethargy, to withdraw into his inner world, inclined to be passive and resigned. A lot of energy is focused on the past in some way. There may be bitter feelings about something, perhaps inadequate mother love." Well, that last bit came up ahead of time!

M: I am impressionable, especially to men, which comes from my father. My dad was the greatest being on earth. (Goes on generally to confirm the statements made.) I do feel easily threatened but women threaten me more than men.

R: Yes, that's in point five. Well, let's jump to point five.

(There's not enough charge on his reaction to point three, the issue of inadequate mother love has come up earlier of its own accord.)

Point 5: "His basic expectations of others tend to be rather fixed and somewhat unrealistic, therefore he is vulnerable to a great deal of disappointment. Particularly tends to idealize women. At the same time, he needs a large circle of friends and needs the support of like-minded others for emotional balance and sexual functioning."

R: Possibly the reason you feel easily threatened by women is that you want so much from them that they can't really give. There seems to be a fantasy that some woman is going to release you from the stuff about your mother and, in fact, no woman is going to be able to do that. So I would invite you to look at what you expect from women.

M: What do I expect from women? At one level I just want to say "nothing, full stop." That's the Tough Guy in me talking. The second level is that there is a side in me that wants to protect women. The women I idealize are women who are soft and sensitive. The other part of that is that I can't really give in to the fact that I might *want* a woman. It's like I can be giving and protective but I can't *take* it from a woman. I'm terribly concerned about the possibility of having my emotions played with.

R:Before we deal with that, let's take in point four, which we skipped, because it's very relevant. "Very strong sexual nature, central to his entire life, but creates many difficulties about it. A basic capacity for an open, warm, natural and harmonious flow of love and sex. Yet distrusts the free flow of feelings. May have the feeling that relationships are so highly emotionally charged that they are potentially destructive and best avoided altogether." It's a problem because there is this very open, soft, generous side of you but it's not okay to let it out. People are going to do something with it; they're going to use it to your disadvantage. So there's a lot of snarl-up around that.

M: There are two things I think about. One is that I always feel that if I could only find people I was at ease with I could let myself out a bit and I could ease off and enjoy myself but it never happens. It's an illusion.

R: It's another "if only."

M: So far, I haven't really had a good, long successful sexual relationship with a woman. I've been prone—I say "prone" because I don't understand it—to having homosexual relationships. I've never understood that— why I should opt for homosexual relationships when I know instinctively inside me that what I really want is a warm, loving sexual relationship with a woman. Yet I keep going the other way. And, going on to this warm, loving side of me—which I know I have somewhere and is another thing I can't access properly—I often transfer those feelings to another man. (He then describes in some detail a recent encounter with another man and says, "I transferred all my soft feelings onto him.")

R: I don't *know* if this is true but it came to me when you were talking and it's something to look at. It looks to me like this. First part: mother is not accessible and that's a nut that the monkey has grabbed. You have to have that be so in order to survive. So, therefore, the sort of woman you could have the kind of relationship you want with is inaccessible too. She's got to be because you're still playing out the stuff with your mother and any woman you get attracted to becomes your mother, for the purposes of the relationship. Remember, just keep looking at that. It's something that you latched on to when God came out of the office with that juicy, dramatic script that he had for you. That bit I'm clear about. The second part of it I'm not so clear about but it looks like you have so much trouble in really owning these warm feelings...

M: I do. I have dreadful problems with that.

R: Right. So you then project them onto other men and get emotionally involved with other men as a way of sort of having your own feelings by proxy.

M: That's the way it is. It took a good friend of mine who is a psychiatrist to point that out to me. I believe him. I believe that's right.

(Something a bit wrong here. It's nice to have my diagnosis confirmed by a psychiatrist but the point of all this was that he had said he didn't understand his homosexual feelings. Now it turns out that he is already aware of the explanation I have suggested. Reading the transcript suggests to me that I may have missed an opportunity here and that I could have confronted him with this anomaly. As it was, I let it pass with the comment that it seemed to be only an intellectual understanding. More talk about this, then he brings up the issue of his mother again. The interview then goes over much the same ground with me pointing out and hammering away at that what he needs to be handling is the paradox of "My life won't work until I can get to my soft feelings and/or get in touch with my feelings about my mother and I can't do that so my life won't work." This is okay and is what usually happens. The resistance of the mind is so great that you need to be prepared to patiently wear it down. [If your own feelings of exasperation or helplessness come up, acknowledge them and allow them to be there.] The dialogue goes on for about 15 minutes, with me constantly bringing him back to the issue and reminding him of the basic framework. I'm omitting it because I don't think it would contribute much to the reader.)

M: Probably the most central issue for me which is coming into my mind more and more is that I don't have any very clear idea who I am. You're telling me to kind of step back and take a look at all the issues in my life and see myself but I don't even know who I'm looking at.

(This is very sophisticated, plausible monkey stuff. If you let yourself believe in it, it could stop the session dead.)

R: OK. Well, put that up on the screen too. "I don't know who the hell I am!"

M: (missing the point completely) Yes, if only I could settle down with who I was...

R: (forcefully, almost shouting) But look! You keep going back to this "if only." What's so for you is that you don't know who the hell you are. So what?

(Trying a shock effect. This time it works. A couple of others in the omitted passage had been ignored. Up to this point Martin has been very much with me but he has been talking about it all in a very reasonable tone as though it were stuff he has been through many times before, as, indeed, he has. An advantage of a client who has done some kind of therapy is that he is familiar with the general process and with the idea of looking at his stuff. The disadvantage is that the stuff itself becomes *too* familiar to him and loses its potential shock value. Now, when Martin replies, his voice sounds more angry and animated.)

M: So what for me is that it feels like a desperate bloody issue. That's so what for me. I almost don't want to speak when I realize I don't know who I am because I've got nothing to say.

R: (matching his tone—it's beginning to sound like a shouting match) Yes. So that's another dog just run across the road. What I'm getting at is that *ultimately* none of these things are a big deal. I mean, sure, they feel like a big deal when we're struggling with them—they feel terrible. From the point of view of your Real Self it isn't a big deal.

M: It feels like an enormous deal for me at the moment. It feels like, "If I don't find out who I am, this is the end of the world."

R: "If only, if only." I think I'll give you an exercise to do. Write out five hundred times, "If only I had it all figured out, my life would be wonderful."

(This is followed by a simmering silence, broken very animatedly by Martin.)

M: What's really boggling my mind is that you're telling me this as if all these things are inherent parts of me. I've been thinking for years that it's my (expletive deleted) parents that are to blame for all of it! (starts to laugh)

R: (mock ironic) Well, sorry about that, Martin! (laughing)

M: (still laughing) I'm boggled because I've been looking in the wrong direction at who's doing what to whom.

(At last the monkey has let go of the nut! The whole thing has lightened up and this is the turning point of the interview though there is still plenty to do to support Martin's "mini-enlightenment" as we shall see.)

R: Really and truly, you've got to get off blaming your parents. It's paradoxical because you are perfectly *justified* in blaming your parents. They didn't know how to handle you and they screwed you up good. That is true. Not because they *wanted* to screw you up but because they were stuck in their hang-ups. If you want to play the blame game, you've got to take it back to Adam and Eve. You've got to step up a level. The desire to blame your parents won't go away—not immediatley, anyway. It's a matter of putting it in the bigger framework of, "I chose this. I created this." There's a bigger and more exciting game to play than being justified about how inept your parents were.

M: But where do I go from here? I'm doing this therapy which almost encourages me to blame my parents.

R: Carry on blaming your parents but do it with awareness. Find out as much as you possibly can about all the ways in which you blame your parents. Get really clear about it. *But quit taking it seriously.* That's the difference.

M: (laughing) I like that! "Quit taking it seriously!" For me it gets to be a life or death issue.

(He is alternating a lot, at this point, between being light and very heavy. On the one hand, he has now really seen that he doesn't have to go on holding on to his old patterns. On the other hand, it feels so unfamiliar and scary not to be holding them, that he will keep picking them up again. This, of course, is what usually happens and this process will go on. If he keeps on being willing to allow the stuff to be and to go on being clear with himself about it, one day he will notice that the business of wanting to get in touch with the stuff about his mother is no longer an issue. As far as I am concerned the main purpose of the session is accomplished. Martin, however, still wants to discuss the issue of taking it seriously.)

R: Let's get really clear about this. I'm not asking you to actually *do* it, to actually stop taking it seriously now. You can't, anyway. You could only put on an act about it, be on a position about it. What I'm asking you to do is to be *willing* to have it be so that ultimately this stuff isn't serious, to create a space for yourself around it. Actually *doing* it may be further down the road for you. Being *willing* to have it be that way you can do now.

M: My answer very clearly is that it feels like one of these days I will be willing but not at the moment.

R: Okay. That's fine. Just notice that you're *not* willing to move off that stuff. Don't make a big deal out of it. That's where you are.

M: It feels very difficult to let go of it.

R: What would happen—what would your life be like if you quit taking all this stuff so seriously?

M: (ruefully) There's a strong possibility that I'd be happy.

R: That would be dreadful, wouldn't it? Somebody once said that human beings would rather be right than be happy and it's true.

M: (laughter again) It's reminded me that there is one thing I can always take not seriously and that's examinations. I might get stewed up about them three or four weeks before but once I walk into the room I refuse to take it as a life or death issue. And I've been very successful in exams.

R: Well, there you are. You know it works.

M: I know it works! You're right. You're very right.

R: Okay, where are you at? What are you going to do? Are you clear about what we've dealt with?

M: My feeling as a whole is that I'll have to go away and play the tape because I've said so much and you've said so much and I can't remember it all... Yet I feel as though I do remember it vividly really.

(Effectively, this is the end of the session. There is a little more reinforcing of the insight and, finally, some straight detailed information giving but the grip of the vicious circle he was in has been loosened. At that level, it doesn't matter whether he remembers the session or not because his "mini-enlightenment" will go on working for him anyway. However, the content of the session is important because it constitutes tools that he can go on using for himself to recreate the experience of the mini-enlightenment and to handle other material as it comes up. As it happened, I saw Martin again two or three days after the session; he remarked, among other things, that being introduced to the notion of "quit taking it seriously" had been an important contribution to his peace of mind.)

PETER: Major Chart Themes

1.   A strong sense of discipline, duty, of being separate from others and having to do things on his own. Rather austere, perfectionist. Feels that life is essentially effort and struggle and is motivated by a need to be seen to be working at it and performing. Very good at getting things done and at inventing new and productive ways of doing them.

2.   Finds it difficult to see a clear course for himself, inclined to drift and yet feels guilty about it because he thinks he should be acting. Sudden swings in moods and sudden failures of energy. Sees many possibilities but does not really like to be committed to any one thing. Therefore liable to grab at courses of action because they relieve tension rather than because they are what he really wants to do.

3.   Very impressionable, is afraid of being conned. Partly for this reason, tends to hold himself aloof from others. Reluctant to get into anything that may mean self-revelation. Basically, an excitable and emotional person but controls this severely. This results in him spending much time living up to what he imagines are other people's expectations rather than being himself.

4.   A need for power and leadership. Expects total loyalty from associates and subordinates but does not, in fact, trust people very much.

Feels that people are not reliable, that they may be full of goodwill and promises but that they do not, and cannot, deliver the goods. At the same time, he is able to have a powerful effect on the people around him. He is a good judge of his audience and can enthuse others by the quality of his own enthusiasm.

5.   As with feelings in general, sexuality is very strong yet he tends to be rather austere about it, disapproving of it at some level in himself and others. He will tend to subordinate sexual needs to duty or other practical

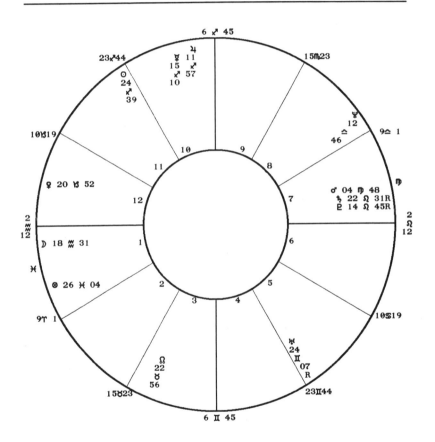

Figure 1.9.2 Peter. Born December 17, 1947 at 10:45 A.M., G.M.T. in Durham City, England. Chart calculated with Topocentric houses. Data from mother's memory. Calculations by Astro-Computing Services.

considerations. At another level, love and sex are experienced as being vital to full functioning and as keys to transformation or self-improvement.

Peter is 34 and a businessman. I am giving here only a short extract from the session. The session is interesting inasmuch as it illustrates two points. One is the bringing out into the light a seemingly unacceptable feeling—hatred for his parents. The second point is that he turned out to have a saboteur subpersonality that almost wrecked the entire session. At one level, it seems to me that I made a good many mistakes and that a result was obtained almost in spite of my efforts rather than because of them. The secret saboteur will usually hook you through your own desire to look good, to try hard and do an especially good job.

I was aware of the possibility of sabotage from the start of the session, but for some reason I didn't confront it directly. Peter was very open, likeable and cooperative with a kind of man-to-man let's get down to business air about him. I was half aware that my reaction to this was to feel that I had to produce something special and impressive and to be particularly down to earth about it. This led me into making heavy use of subpersonality theory, which is something I rarely do because the notion of subpersonalities can become too concrete. This is what happened here. We identified, and strongly reactivated, a subpersonality which we called Sulky Kid. It was a nice, clear, nitty-gritty concept, and my own mistaken sense of what was wanted led me to emphasize it far too much and so to give it a great deal of mass. Incredibly, I even let pass the signals in point three of the chart themes. As I was reading out "...afraid of being conned...Reluctant to get into anything that may mean self-revelation," I even commented to Peter that we might need to handle that in terms of the actual session.

The session took place in the evening after a fairly full day and I was rather tired. Peter seemed so cooperative and relaxed that I was readily persuaded that there was no need for a direct confrontation at such an early stage of the interview. There are a lot of things I might have done differently, but I think that one of the main values of this transcript is that it clearly demonstrates the power of giving up the need to be right. Quite late in the session, when I had thought the job was more or less finished, the Sulky Kid turns on me and attempts to invalidate the entire method of working. There is a point in the dialogue at which Peter, or, rather, Sulky Kid in Peter, challenges me to defend and prove what I'm doing intellectually. It would have been very easy to get into that, and if I had done so, I would have gone headlong into the trap. I would have wound up feeling clumsy, incompetent and a fraud. Peter, presumably, would have gone away feeling conned, cheated and generally justified in his view that nothing is really going to help him make any changes in his life.

Though I was considerably disconcerted by the developments, I retained enough awareness of what I was doing to allow the attack to be there and to treat it as just something that was coming up and invite Peter to look at it in that light. Eventually, as Peter puts it, the impetus to attack the validity of what has been done disappears. It isn't that it has been argued down and that he has been convinced or persuaded of anything. It is that we were both accepting it and allowing it to be and it moved to destruction. In fact this part of the dialogue is as clear an illustration of something moving to destruction within a session as one would be likely to get.

The interview began with some fairly lively discussion of points 1 and 2. It was good ground clearing but nothing came up that seemed to invite going after. What got it moving was the statement in point 3 that he was basically excitable and emotional but controlled it severely. This brought up a lot of childhood stuff. His parents were always too busy to pay any attention to him so he was seething with rage and frustration about this. What made it worse was that he was forbidden to express any feelings at all. Peter recalled wanting to run around tearing up the account books that always seemed more important than him to his parents and to scream "I hate you lot," and being afraid to do it. The hatred was for his parents and also for the business. Hating such an intangible entity seems to have contributed to a great deal of frustration.

R: What's happened to that hatred now?

P: Quite! Well, I mean...I think it must...it must still be inside.

(Hardly a clear owning of it but a fair start.)

R: Yes. I think that's one of the nuts the monkey's still holding. (long pause) Who do you hate? What I'm after is to get you to allow yourself to have the hatred, without judging yourself about it.

P: The hatred is certainly for my parents' business so it's something intangible. It was the whole thing in which we lived. This thing that took all their time—or, rather, that they gave all their time to. I have hatred for my parents' business and hatred for them too because they were so stupid as to give all their time to it and none to me.

R: I think what's happened is that, at some point, you created all this hatred and it's not acceptable and you can't express it so you resist it and go unconscious of it and it's stuck in the maintenance phase. So there's a lot of hate that you need to allow yourself to have and to look at in a nonjudgmental way. Can you do that—bearing in mind that a lot of stuff will come up around it. Especially guilt, maybe. You know—"I *shouldn't* feel this way about my parents who slaved their fingers to the bone for me."

P: (laugh of recognition) It's difficult to do it just here.

R: Well, it's as good a place as any—in fact, better than most. I'm not asking you to let go of the whole thing now. I'm asking you to see it up on the screen.

P: I can see it up on the screen all right.

R: That's all you have to do. Part of the difficulty with this is that we're so conditioned to think that we have to fix things. All we have to do is tell the truth about it and it processes out. The bottom line of it is that you hate your parents.

P: There are two totally opposed feelings. The other is a part of me that is full of joy and wants to be really outgoing yet there's this barrier stopping him all the time.

R: What's the barrier consist of?

(Always get the client to be as specific as possible.)

P: It's like a jelly round me.

R: What's the jelly saying to you?

P: Something like, "You can't respond to this; mother won't like it."

R: What about, "I'm not going to respond to this because I'm going to prove to my parents how wrong they are to treat me in this way. I'm going to spend my entire life proving my parents are wrong."

P: Mm. That's what I don't like to admit, of course. That's where the hatred comes in. That's how the hatred of them comes into operation. And I won't let go of it. (pause) And yet that's stupid.

R: Yes. (both laugh)

P: So where does that stupidity come from? Why am I so stupid?

R: It's the monkey again.

P: Yes, it's the hatred, isn't it? Unless the hatred is expressed the stupidity is going to stay.

(This is a common belief that keeps people stuck. It isn't expressing the hatred that allows it to move, it is taking responsibility for having the hatred. This is the encounter group fallacy. People express and cathart negative feelings and they feel a little better for a while but the basic pattern doesn't change. Martin, in the last transcript, is an instance of this; he had been doing a cathartic type of therapy.)

R: It doesn't have to be *expressed*. It needs to be told the truth about—which is what you're doing now. Would you be willing to have that hatred clear up out of your life? Would you be willing to give up getting back at your parents?

P: Part of me wouldn't.

R: Exactly, that's the honest answer. The thing is just to notice that. If you'd said "yes" I'd have been suspicious.

P: Yet that is what we are all moving towards in the fullness of time. When we say "take responsibility for my actions," that's what we mean.

(I'm not quite sure what he is saying here. He is intellectualizing a lot and I don't feel that he is really getting that all he has to do is acknowledge his stuff. I try to go for some action rather than talk.)

R: What I want you to get is that what counts is being *willing* and you can do that now, this minute. You can't suddenly decide to be responsible for your life. Apart from anything else there is this part of you that would rather go through another fifteen incarnations getting back at your parents for handling you so badly. It's more "I'm willing to *assume* that I'm responsible. I'm willing to play the game by that rule." Can you do that?

P: You mean to say that, "I am willing to be responsible for my actions as much as I can...that gives me a cop-out, doesn't it..."as much as I can"?

(His Real Self keeps breaking through but to acknowledge it would mean letting go of the hatred, which he is not willing to do.)

R: I'm not saying *realize* your responsibility. I'm saying, "Are you willing to come from that position?"

P: I can put it in the future. I'm willing to be responsible for my actions...next year.

(I'm not asking him to be willing to be responsible for his *actions* only but for his life. I'm unwilling to confront his use of words at this point because I sense that doing so would lead us into an abstract intellectual discussion, which is not what I want.)

R: That's no good. Are you willing to do it now? You will not get many better opportunities for getting off it than you've got right this minute. I'm not asking you to give up your hatred—far from it; in fact, I want you to explore it and get to really know it—I'm asking you to put it into a broader framework.

P: To be responsible for that hatred?

R: Yes, that it's there because you intended it to be there. And you intended it to be there because when God came out of the office with that script under his arm, he said, "Peter, you're going to get to hate your parents." *Lovely, juicy drama.*

P: But why should I want to do it?

(Monkey, monkey, monkey. His mind is looking for reasons and he is not allowing himself to see the actual picture.)

R: There is no reason. To handle this stuff you have to accept that you did it because you did it. Otherwise you can go on finding reasons for hating your parents, then reasons for the reasons and then reasons for those and so on and on. And, meanwhile, you're still stuck in hating them, with all the effect that has on every other area of your life.

P: But having that hatred does save me being responsible for my actions. And part of me wants to carry on with it.

R: Yes, but this is all the monkey, Peter. Just look at what's going on. The monkey is kicking and screaming to hold onto hating your parents. All this looking for reasons and analyzing and discussing it is pure mind. It's survival. You got programmed, if you like, or, to look at it another way, you bought into the notion that having suppressed hatred for your parents is what you have to do in order to survive.

(We went back over the ground of his childhood circumstances and it became evident that the part of him that had the suppressed hatred and was withholding from the world could be likened to a sulky child. Peter latched onto it as something that made his patterns easier to see. With some relief I went along with this and for about thirty minutes we looked at what was going on in terms of the Sulky Kid subpersonality. Earlier, when we were going through point 1 of the chart themes, I had suggested that that part of him was a kind of John Wayne figure, which had appealed to him considerably. He now started to see that a lot of his life was a conflict between John Wayne and Sulky Kid. This was a valid insight but unproductive to become stuck in.

Subpersonality theory has largely been developed by the Psychosynthesis school of therapy, founded by Roberto Assagioli. The basic idea is that we consist of many different personalities, each with their own needs, wants and view of the world. Some of the subpersonalities are supportive of each other, some are in conflict, as is the case here between John Wayne and Sulky Kid. In daily life, we identify with one after the other of the subpersonalities, more or less unconsciously. Subpersonality theory is a powerful cognitive tool. Its danger is that paying a lot of attention to a subpersonality can overenergize it, as happens here. Also, there is a tendency for people to use it *not* to be responsible for their lives in the same way that many people use astrology. It is just as easy to get into the position "It's not me, it's my Victim subpersonality" as it is to get into "It's not me, it's my Neptune."

For these reasons, I seldom make much use of subpersonality theory. It seemed to me that doing so in Peter's case was assisting us to greater clarity about what was going on. Indeed it was, but there was a price to be paid.)

P: Does the Sulky Kid take on such importance with everyone? I can't see what's stopping everybody else from getting on.

R: It's different in different people but we all have something like it. The emphasis is different but most people go through their lives trying to prove how wrong their parents were for not giving it to us exactly the way we wanted it.

(Nothing wrong with this statement but I failed to see where it was leading. Fortunately, the idea of confronting whatever comes up as being grist to the mill was well enough established to enable us to avoid complete disaster.)

P: I felt a curious letdown when I realized everybody else is suffering the Sulky Kid syndrome. [This is not true and not what I've actually said but I didn't want to get into a dispute about words so I let it pass.] I feel like I've been through the brief now. This is the introduction to the Sulky Kid. That's what this therapy is about. Introduction to the Sulky Kid...ah, Sulky Kid speaking again here.

R: He's going to try to invalidate all this.

P: What's going on now is that I'm thinking, "This guy's approach is to introduce people to their Sulky Kid. He's got that one pat."

R: As a matter of fact you're the first person for a long time that I've used that particular notion with. But it is true that most of us have this kind of Sulky Kid pattern.

(I am really disconcerted at this point, completely hooked into being right and justifying my handling of the session. I'm even saying something that isn't true. We don't all have a *Sulky* Kid. We do all have a Rejected or Hurt Child subpersonality, but it isn't necessarily sulky.)

P: (suspiciously) So, what are the other patterns if it isn't the Sulky Kid.

(Notice the complete breakdown of communication. I have just, incorrectly, said that it *is* the Sulky Kid. He is really out to get me. Hostility is underlying his words. He—or his saboteur subpersonality—is basically accusing me of operating from a flip and shallow "Sulky Kid" formula and dressing it up with astrology. I am floundering badly at this point and very stuck in the need to be right, with the breakdown of communication. I have him do an exercise of imagining putting all his stuff into a basket and letting go of it. This seems to work briefly, when Peter reports feelings of clarity and not manipulating. I am just starting to relax when Sulky Kid returns to the fray. Throughout all this, I am stuck in being right. I'm feeling that my own survival is threatened and I have really used the exercise to try to make Peter wrong for challenging me.)

P: The feeling I got when I discovered everyone has something like this is still there. (long pause) I feel as though I've been given a spiel—can you imagine it, I feel as though I've been given a spiel—that everyone else is going to get, and has had, using the vehicle of an astrological chart.

(We get into a heavy discussion again about the ways in which people are different and the ways in which they aren't, with me trying to get Peter to see that none of this is the point and that the issue is what *he* is going to do about his patterns. I am recovering from the attack a little and gradually letting go of my need to be right.)

P: Yes, we all do function on very similar human traits. But this Sulky Kid is fighting very hard at the moment.

R: I can see that. And the thing is not to resist it but to look at what's going on now as a really great opportunity to find out more about it, letting it have more space. So, I encourage you to be your Sulky Kid as much as you like.

(I have got off needing to be right now and I can see the conflict as being more within Peter than between us.)

P: (long pause) But I still have the feeling that I've been given something that everybody else would get and that's what I want to get through.

R: You feel you've been given a snow job?

P: The Sulky Kid does. *I* want to know. I want to see that isn't right.

R: I can't answer that. If I were to spend the next couple of hours going through charts and explaining how different cases *are* different, I'd never be able to prove it to you. You've just got to look at it as something that the Sulky Kid is putting up.

(He never got what he wanted from his parents so he won't get what he wants from me. The only way to get through it is to have him confront that. It might have been useful to have said so more explicitly.)

P: But he's going to invalidate the whole session if he doesn't get the answer to that one.

R: Let's be clear about this. What is it that you don't feel you've got out of the session that you had some idea you would get?

P: I'd perhaps hoped to see some aspect of the Sulky Kid in operation.

R: Well, you've certainly got that. You can see the little devil going away like crazy right now.

P: Yes, I can see the whole of him, in that sense...Okay, I'm going to walk out of here with the observation of a Sulky Kid. Every now and again, John Wayne's going to come in and try to kick him out. And there'll be feelings of guilt and doing too much, then doing too little and all the rest of it. And I'll be able to observe it.

R: Great.

P: But I still want to know, is somebody else going to come in here tomorrow and walk out with the same feelings.

R: What if they do? It's *your* feelings that we're concerned about. It's possible that I might have another client with near enough the same chart as yours.

P: Well, my key words are "Sulky Kid," right?

R: Hold on. It just so happens that it's been convenient to use the concept of a sulky kid. It might be that the best thing you could possibly do is forget those words. The fact that you're visualizing that Sulky Kid so strongly and are so fixed on it is going on maintaining it.

(A belated comment. If I'd made this point 20 or 30 minutes earlier, I might have saved a lot of hassle. Then again, I might not. This is a really tricky subpersonality to deal with.)

P: "Old Self" in other words.

R: Whatever you like to call it. The essential thing, whether or not we call him Sulky Kid, is that there is a part of you that really believes that in order to survive you have to have your life screwed up. That's what you need to be looking at.

P: I'm with you. The reason of this session is to show that one doesn't have to hang on to one's preconceived ideas.

R: Yes. Also, you won't really know what value you've got out of this session until you've seen it working. It might be days or weeks.

(True, though a little defensive on my part.)

P: How could one nurture this session?

R: One thing is to use the tape; that's what it's really for. But the main thing right now is that if you feel you've been given a snow job, go on looking at that, that it's been a snow job. Because when I say, "Look at everything that comes up," I mean that absolutely literally. If that's what's there for you, the best way to nurture the session and get the value from it is to go on looking at "I've been given a snow job," paradoxical as that may sound.

P: Actually, the impetus has gone from that.

R: Great, but if it should come back, then just observe it along with the other stuff.

P: It really does loosen these things up to talk about them.

● ● ●

We did get a substantial amount of work done, though the transcript is obviously not meant to be a model of how to do it. Peter's angry, hurt conviction that he will never get proper support from anyone, which is evident in his feelings of being emotionally neglected by his parents, did get handled, largely by being acted out on me. Ideally, I could have spotted it earlier—it is perfectly plain to see, in retrospect—and made it the main feature of a confrontation. In that way, we would have had more time and energy to explore it thoroughly and I would not have had to have so much of my attention on merely maintaining control of the session.

However, this difficult session seems to me to illustrate some important points better than a smooth running one would. Particularly, as I have said, it illustrates the power inherent in not having to be right and accepting nonjudgmentally whatever the client comes up with. It also illustrates the point that you have to be prepared constantly to be conscious of whatever is going on in you and accepting of it. I realize now that Peter was plugging me in to some unresolved stuff of my own in the same general area. Although, in the comments, I have indicated how I might have done things differently, in practice I had no choice but to do it the way I did.

It is useful to think of every session as being an encounter between two Real Selves that has to operate through the vehicles of the two egos. It is as though the Real Selves of Peter and myself were determined to get the work done in spite of all the mistakes that our egos made. We eventually got to where we intended to be. The fact that we made what might be seen as an unnecessary detour through very rough country doesn't really have any bearing on the end result.

BARBARA: Major Chart Themes

1.   Need for a stable, nurturing relationship. Tends to idealize love and affection, perhaps because of a childhood lack. Expects love to be transforming—a yearning for something unattainable.

2. Does not trust groups very much; tends to be private and withdrawn, likes order and routine. Feelings frozen below a certain level. Tends to be a loner. Needs other people's respect and approval but prefers to keep them at an emotional distance.

3. Has a great capacity for success and fulfillment with, possibly, some unusual powers and resources and considerable charisma. Nevertheless, success is elusive. She has a sense that nothing really works—inclined to give up out of exhaustion and frustration.

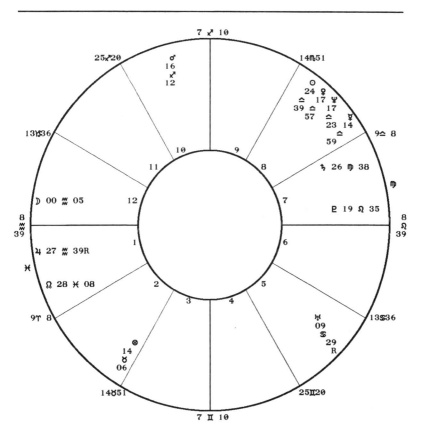

Figure 1.9.3 Barbara. Born October 18, 1950 at 3:36 P.M., B.S.T., in London, England. Data from mother's memory and the chart has presumably been rectified. The non-rectified time was not given. Calculations by Astro-Computing Services.

4. Very active, forceful, courageous but feels isolated, as though she has to run on willpower and endurance alone. Can accomplish much through powerful self-discipline. Inclined to see life in terms of conquest and competition.

5. Deep, chronic dissatisfaction with love and sex. The pattern is of needing to experience that certain things don't work for her in order to discover the things that do.

6. The importance of sexual love is highly emphasized. There may be a conscious or unconscious expectation that it will automatically be ecstatic and wonderful. At the same time, loving and being loved is somehow perceived as unsafe.

This was a follow-up session. I had seen Barbara for the first time about six weeks previously. On the face of it, she is the kind of woman who seems to have everything going for her. She is a career woman, very intelligent, with a prestigious job, and extremely attractive in both looks and personality. When making the appointment she had specifically stated that she wanted to look at the issues of her difficulties in forming satisfying relationships with men.

During the first session, we examined the chart themes and it became evident that the contextual one was number 2. She was very resistant in that she attempted all the time to keep the session at the level of entertaining intellectual discussion, at which she was very adept. She talked readily enough but it was all on the level of anecdote, explanation and justification, with little or no emotional content and almost impersonal, as though she were presenting a case history with copious footnotes. Astrologically, we have Aquarius ascendant quincunx Uranus, Mercury in Libra square Uranus, sesquiquadrate Jupiter.

We quickly identified a belief system that love was unattainable, which she recognized at an intellectual level with no trouble. Almost the whole of the session was then spent in attempting to get through the layer of explanation and justification. In answer to my question "Would you be willing to have genuine love in your life?" she replied, "I don't know what love is." This had the feel of being a genuine experience and not just a concept, and that seemed to be about as far as we were going to get. I had her look at the experience and invited her to be willing to accept and stay with the not-knowing.

In the interval, she had the experience of getting, at a gut, emotional level, that she became involved with men who behaved badly to her and that she was no longer willing to go on doing that and putting up with it. This, itself, is a good example of how the process works. A piece of insight and clarity gained in the session creates more insight and clarity which, in turn, needs simply to be allowed to be there. I will quote the subsequent session at some length. It is rather discursive and repetitious but this type of discursiveness is a very common form of resistance and so is worth examining. It is tricky to deal with because if you try to clamp down on it too early you will probably simply upset and alienate the client to no purpose. The thing to do is to accept it, allow it to be and stay alert for some opportunity of engaging the client's feelings. In the first session, Barbara had talked herself to the edge of tears—which she suppressed on the grounds that they would spoil her makeup—before getting to the realization that she didn't know what love was. Barbara is, in fact, rather an extreme example of this type of resistance. On a scale of 1 to 10, where 10 is impossible to work with at all, I would rate her about 7, maybe 7½.

R: The crunch point of the last session was you saying "I don't know what love is." We got to a quick intellectual recognition of the issue, which was "Love is unattainable," and the rest of the session was about having you experience that. You did get it experientially but it was right at the end and there was a lot of monkey stuff to wrestle with.

B: Right. I felt very good about things after that session, and I felt quite "up" for the rest of the day and had some interesting dreams.

(Continues with a very detailed account of a girl in the dream who seems very self-possessed and who, in the dream, was standing up to Barbara's father in a way that she would like to do herself.)

R: (rather groping for some point of contact) Did you feel overwhelmed by your father?

B: He's very emotional although he makes out to be very reasonable. (Longish description of her father, including details of his chart—she has a sound knowledge of astrology.)

R: Okay, let's pin down what you said. It's "I'm not allowed to be me" for one thing and also, "If I am myself something terrible's going to happen."

B: I've been reading some books recently and... (much detail and justification, not responding to my statement. The only clear thing that comes out of it is Barbara saying that she gets very guilty and upset about people who like her and have expectations of her. This is remotely connected with her earlier statements about her father. She seems to be disowning her power to have any effect on men at all, as far as I can make out.)

R: Well, this needs a bit of sorting out. It may be true that you *do* attract men who fall head over heels in love with you and who will go berserk if you say "no." That might be a reality, I don't know.

B: (embarrassed) No, I don't think that really does happen.

(Very anxious to disown her own power. I am going along with the interaction at this "chat" level because I don't feel sure enough of the rapport to push it any harder and to be more confronting, though I am going to have to be more confronting sooner or later if we are going to get anything useful accomplished.)

B: I tend to attract emotional misfits.

R: Yes, you said that last time. I should think emotional misfits would be very likely to feel rejected by you.

B: I don't know. I seem to attract emotional misfits who reject me; I don't know if they feel rejected by me.

R: We seem to be getting on to something else that we got on to in the last session, which is your unwillingness to accept how wonderful you are.

B: (embarrassed laugh) Yes...Okay...fair enough!

R: And it ties up, for me, with the whole business to do with your father.

B: (evading the issue completely) Let me tell you what happened to me since I saw you, before we go any further...I need to spend about five minutes telling you about this person because that'll make you realize why I got this sort of revelation.

R: Just tell me what the revelation is.

B: (falling over herself) Well...it's hard...no, I can't...it's...it's...I mean, I didn't really have...I didn't...I can't! It'll only work if I tell you what happened.

R: Hang on a minute because this is relevant. I'm very much aware that it's really difficult for you to say something without justifying it. I'm pretty sure you don't need to spend five minutes explaining and justifying your revelation. I will get it, if you just tell me what it is.

B: Well, okay. As a result of the way he was behaving, I realized that what I'd been doing was compensating for the behavior of the people I like. You've said I tend to attract people who behave badly and unreasonably [from the chart] and I do. And I had this revelation at a gut level that I've been allowing behavior in men whom I'm even slightly sexually attracted to that I'd never tolerate in girlfriends. Having realized that, I got very upset because I thought that now I'd realized that and I wasn't going to tolerate it anymore there was absolutely *nothing* left.

(After this straight talking, she goes into a confused account of getting drunk at a party and having some further realization in a car. It's not that she doesn't know what she's trying to say; it is that there is such a heavy taboo on trusting herself and allowing herself to be and to know what she knows. The impulse to justify rather than confront makes her temporarily incoherent.)

B: ...and, going back in the car...and I would not have been talking had I not been...because I got to the party and I was fed up because...I decided to get drunk...it was a dumb thing to do, bad Neptune aspects...anyway...

R: When you listen to this tape...

B: (laughing) No, no, I'm never going to listen to it.

R: ...just notice how much you justify and explain.

B: Fine. Going back in the car, I was crying and they said, "Why are you so upset?" and I said, "Because I'm never going to get laid again!" [Said with a sort of rueful humor that put me in mind of someone like Goldie Hawn.] And the people I was with didn't understand. They thought I was upset with a particular man, but I wasn't.

(This is another illustration of the process in action. She has had a paradoxical pattern of "In order to get love and to survive, I have to put up with bad behavior from men," putting up with unloving behavior, in fact. Now she is confronting it—having a gut level experience of it—and the basic unlovedness is coming up. Things look as though they are getting worse. She then goes on to describe something that happened soon after her revelation in which a man was behaving badly to her and she had to be very direct about her needs.)

B: What I ended up getting at a gut level is that I'm not going to put up with this lousy behavior any longer. But I feel now as though there's nothing, there's nothing there at all.

R: The pattern looks to me something like this. It's not okay for you to be the way you are. It's not okay for you to be wonderful. It's not okay for you to come out into the world and just be Barbara. Listen to the tape. There's about ten minutes of justification for every ten seconds of direct statement.

B: I've been told that by so many people...

R: Well, it's okay. Just let it be there. And the monkey has grabbed hold of a nut that goes, "If I squash myself down and if I have people behave badly to me, I can get away with it." Now you're starting to see that pattern and you've moved off it. It's not running you now. But the emptiness underneath it, the feeling of "I'm *never* going to get love" has now come up.

B: I'm sure it's just a stage but it *feels* lousy.

R: Yes, it does. It feels awful when you're in it.

B: I've never had this at a gut level before. I've seen it intellectually.

R: You are in a transition stage at the moment. You can see clearly that the way you've been handling your relationships with men doesn't work, but you have't yet moved on to discovering what *does* work. How long it will take you to do that depends on your willingness to have it work.

B: It's hard to know what to do. I don't know what to do.

(This is a covert "Tell me how to fix it.")

N: No, that's it. You don't know what to do. Are you willing not to know what to do?

B: Well, I suppose...Part of the reason I've been getting better about love is that my work is going well and I've been getting good feedback on it. Which helps me feel more okay as a person and less willing to accept other people's evaluations of me in other areas.

(She has to justify and find a reason for everything. It is pure mind stuff, pure monkey. She is also still seeing herself as the effect of other people's opinions.)

R: Can you now take a big jump and *choose* to be okay as a person, irrespective of what sort of feedback you get?

B: ...I get very upset if I invest part of myself in someone and they don't respond. It's not just a sexual thing because it happens with girlfriends as well.

R: There is a real, basic, horrible loneliness that you're not really confronting. It started to come up after the party. It's a very unpleasant thing to confront but that's what's there. It's coming up now. The thing you need to be doing is looking at how you come out of a total context of loneliness. The way you get through it is by accepting it and getting beyond the whole thing as something you created. And when you're doing it, it will be very unpleasant indeed because all the emptiness and loneliness will come up. Waking up at three o'clock in the morning and feeling terrible and all that stuff.

B: It's like the eight of swords.

(The tarot card. In the Rider deck, it depicts a grief-stricken woman sitting up in bed.)

R: It sounds horrible and it is horrible but there are two levels of reality.

B: You've got to bottom out and start climbing again.

R: It isn't even that. It's a matter of getting to another perspective about the whole thing.

(I repeat the Real Self/actor analogy. She is not really getting it. Notice how she has totally avoided my invitation to choose to be okay.)

R: I want you to go up a level. When you can look at something clearly, really tell the truth to yourself about it, just have it be there, it goes down the drain. It will no longer be an issue for you. And it's not usually that there's a flash and a bang and a big revelation. It's more likely that you will just notice, one day, that you aren't lonely, and haven't been for weeks. It's a very natural process.

(She doesn't really get it and comes up with a lot of resistance by denying the generality of it, talking about her busy social life, with the typical indignation. She is still hardly giving herself time to hear what I say, coming back with an immediate riposte.)

B: It's impossible for me to see beyond loneliness.

R: Yes, when you're stuck in it it *is* impossible to see beyond it. Are you willing to be in that space?

(She comes back with a long anecdote which completely avoids the issue. I let her do it, it still doesn't feel quite appropriate to have a really direct confrontation about the evasiveness. There is a long discussion which basically goes over the same ground we have already covered.)

R: The basic thing that is absolutely yelling at me, out of what you are saying and out of the chart, is that you won't allow yourself to be wonderful. You don't have permission to be wonderful because, if you are, your parents won't love you. The whole thing comes down to that. And all the anecdotes and the drama and the justification is a way of not looking at it.

B: But I keep telling you how well I'm handling it but (shouting) I'm *still* not getting laid, goddamit!

R: (also shouting) Yes! Exactly! Thank God we've got that point made!

(I've been trying to get her to see at a gut level that all the figuring out that she has been doing about her reactions to men is interesting enough in one way but it isn't getting any results. I'm not taking a position one way or the other about whether she should have a sexual relationship again or not. I don't know what would be right for her and neither does she, at this point.)

R: I'm not interested in having you analyze and speculate and figure it out. It's entertaining and it keeps you busy but it doesn't get you anywhere. What I am interested in having you do is move off all that and have a relationship that works for you—on all levels. The way you do it is by just *getting* what's there. You already know this. You've seen it working in the last few weeks. What you've got in your life is this stuff about you're not allowed to be wonderful, you're not allowed to have love.

B: (Brushing it aside) Another thing I feel strongly about and maybe this is justifying but...I mean...sorry, I won't apologize.

R: "Sorry, I won't apologize!?"

B: (Laughing) Oh, that's classic.

R: If you don't allow yourself to be wonderful you won't get the kind of love you want, because what I mean by wonderful is being able to come out into the world and have your life work for you. And there's all this stuff from your parents in the way; you can't be you, you have to be the way they say you have to be. (A reference to material from the earlier session.) At the moment, we're just not getting to confront that. That's okay, as long as you realize it.

(We then get into a discussion about Barbara's relationship with her parents followed by a discussion of the difficulties of being a woman in a man's world—all of it at an intellectual level.)

R: People will take you at your own evaluation. You really do get back what you put in. It comes back to the same thing over again. If you want people to behave decently to you, *you've* got to acknowledge that you're bright and pretty and it's okay for you to put yourself out into the world and it's okay for you to have love relationships.

B: Why do people spend so much time getting back at their parents?

R: (half exasperated, half joking) Do you *ever* listen to anything I say?

B: I do listen to what you say. I'm sorry.

R: Don't apologize for it, just notice that you immediately bat the ball back over the net.

B: (pause) Well, I can't just sit here and say, "Yes, you're right. I *am* wonderful."

R: Why not?

B: Because I don't feel that. I could say it but it would be a pose.

R: But you don't even address the issue. You are doing now because I've stopped you, but mostly you immediately go off on a tangent onto something else, intellectualizing about why this and why that.

B: (long sigh) Oh, dear. (long pause) Now I can't think of anything to say.

R: Great! (pause) It's okay not to be able to think of anything to say.

(As often happens on this sort of occasion, I wish I had a video recording going so that I could give her visual feedback on the difference in the way she looks. The bright, cocktail party armoring has gone. Her expression is much softer; she relaxes, almost slumps, into the sofa she is sittting on and there is a much greater sense of power and presence about her. For the first time in a total of almost four hours of dialogue, I feel that we are really communicating. There is a long silence and I let her sit in it, making no attempt to get her off the hook.)

B: (something inaudible)

R: Embarrassing, isn't it?

B: It is, yes. I can't just sit here and be okay. I've got to justify what I'm doing.

R: You really are going to have to handle that embarrassment and have it be okay to be embarrassed...It's awful. (pause) That's what it boils down to. You're too embarrassed to be who you really are.

(There is a further long silence. When Barbara speaks, she sounds different; she is speaking more slowly and there is some kind of emotion in her voice.)

B: I'm not trying to intellectualize, but why is it that people try to spite their parents? Is it that my parents didn't love me for what I was, so if I end up being what they wanted me to be does that prove that I'm not really lovable?

R: We do it because some of the basic experience is frightening and horrible. A kid comes into the world wanting and needing unconditional love. And she doesn't get it, there are conditions on it. "Grow up and become a Ph.D., and then we'll love you—otherwise no dice." That's not much good to a little kid. And we get very angry about it.

(She rather quickly partially returns to the bright, talkative persona. The session continues for about 20 minutes, with me leading it back to the need to confront the embarrassment.)

R: As we go on talking, it becomes more evident to me that what stands between you and having what you want is sheer embarrassment. It sounds like such a trivial thing but it's terrible. I think more people hang themselves up out of embarrassment than for any other reason. It's more insidious than fear, even.

(Barbara then comes back to the difficulties of being a woman in a man's world—"You've either got to be wimp or a bitch."—and how much energy she and other women put into just coping with this, leaving little left over for what they want to do.)

R: I really understand that but, eventually, it boils down to you not letting you win. Those guys out there who are making it so difficult for you are just demonstrating the inner conflict. They are acting out your expectations for yourself. And you can always find really good, cogent, unarguable reasons why you are not going to win. The thing is, would you be willing to let yourself win?

B (very firmly and clearly) Yes!

(This is as far as we are going to get in this session. She has had enough of an authentic experience of herself for it to move some more of the emotional blockage.)

● ● ●

Of these three sessions, Martin's is probably the nearest to being a typical one, so far as there is such a thing. Peter and Barbara are unusually difficult, for very different reasons. With Peter, it was not so much the fact of the latent hostility itself that made the session difficult but that I got hooked into something of my own and failed to spot it. I had no similar sense of being threatened and challenged with Barbara. The difficulty was exactly the opposite. It would have been all too easy to have let the session become an enjoyable and entertaining chat. I have commented earlier that it tends to be men who get into the detail and justification, so Barbara is something of an exception to this tendency.

Reading a transcript, one can always, with hindsight, see ways in which one might have done the session differently. It seems to me that I might have confronted Barbara with her evasiveness earlier. I was nervous of the possibility of merely alienating her. If, like Martin, she had had some previous experience of therapy, I probably would have confronted her with it earlier as I could have safely assumed that she knew the rules of the game and would not have taken offense. As it was, it felt appropriate to do it when I did and it was certainly effective.

I see my function as being threefold. The first part of it is to provide clients with accurate information about themselves that will stir up the energy connected with the issues they need to be examining. The second function is to provide a sort of combined mirror and focusing device so that they can see what is there for them. The third, and equally important, function is to create a kind of psychic incinerator into which clients can throw their garbage. To just go on accepting what the client is saying and actively listening to it, in a nonjudgmental way, actually destroys it. In Barbara's case, the need to explain and justify was weakened enough so that it was possible to throw the whole thing into reverse gear.

Between doing Barbara's session and typing up the transcript, I heard a radio program about Sappho, the Greek woman poet who lived about 600 BC. I was struck forcefully by the sheer directness of her poetry—the nakedness of it, as one of the presenters of the program described it. It seems to be a beautiful example of what I am constantly trying to get my clients to do—to tell the simple, direct truth about themselves. Contrast Barbara's statements—or the statements of almost any of us—with Sappho's description of her sexual feelings:

> If I meet
>
> you suddenly, I can't
>
> speak—my tongue is broken;
> a thin flame runs under
> my skin; seeing nothing,
>
> hearing only my own ears
> drumming, I drip with sweat;
> trembling shakes my body
>
> and I turn paler than
> dry grass. At such times
> death isn't far from me*

I don't know whether Sappho's love was returned or not, but I have every confidence that she wouldn't have made a big problem out of it, not when she could speak of it so clearly and vividly.

*Mary Barnard, *Sappho: A New Translation*, Berkeley: University of California Press, 1958. Poem 39.

PART

II

Astrology
as a Tool for Understanding:
The Basic Principles

1

Twelve Principles

Interpretation does not play much part in the client interview in the method of counseling outlined in this book. Rather, the interpretation of the chart provides the raw material for the interview, and I have suggested that it is best done ahead of time and reduced to some form of written notes. This is not always possible. Sometimes a client has to be seen on short notice, with hardly enough time to draw up the chart, let alone make written notes on it. These interviews can be more difficult because you have to extract the raw material and put it to use at the same time and without the benefit of a complete overview of the chart which unhurried study makes possible.

Both for these sort of emergencies and for more general reasons, it is desirable for the astrologer to have a fluent understanding of the symbols he is using at as abstract a level as possible. For one thing, it is necessary to understand chart factors as they apply at a psychological level. The more concrete, externalized, fortune-telling meanings will rarely be appropriate in this type of work. Also, the firmer one's grasp of the roots of the symbolism one is using, the more confidence one can have in the accuracy of the interpretations. Sometimes it is necessary to explore a particular area of a person's life in detail, and the more abstract the meanings you use, the broader area you can cover and the greater the chance of getting to the essence of the problem.

For example, if your client's physical environment seems to be an issue in some way and your understanding of the 4th house is limited to home and family, you may not be able to do much more than reflect back to him, in astrological language, what he is saying anyway. If you understand the house as the experience—or the lack of it—of a secure, supported self-image, you can draw him away from being stuck in the physical circumstances. Again, understanding Saturn simply as restriction and limitation does not give very much scope. If it is understood as the drive to maintain existing belief systems, and as one phase in a total process, you have much more room to maneuver.

Probably most people learn astrology by learning keywords for the meanings of the planets, signs and houses. This is an excellent way of getting a practical grasp of what is a very complex subject. Using the keyword method, one can learn to interpret a chart in a few months. From the point of view of giving the student something to work with so that he can check out the basic rules in his own experience, this is fine. I doubt very much whether my own initial interest in astrology would have been nurtured and sustained if I had not learned it in this way. However, it does create the impression of astrology being a set of rather arbitrary and unrelated factors and gives the student little sense of the organic unity of the subject. Without this sense of organic unity, the student also has no sense of the basic underlying principles of interpretation. He is more or less compelled to accept that, for example, Mars means assertion and personal will without being able to see *why* it should mean that in the overall scheme of things and without, therefore, being able to extend and expand this meaning as he may need to do as his own work develops.

Fortunately, since Dane Rudhyar's seminal writings, a great deal of work has been done on clarifying the structure of astrological symbolism and on redefining astrology in terms more appropriate for psychological counseling. What follows is largely intended to be a convenient summary of the work that has been done. It aims to present astrological symbolism as a set of very basic principles with their own inherent logic. It is not so much that one will often want to use these notions directly in working with a client—though sometimes it is useful to be able to do so—as that they provide a solid basis of understanding. Somebody once said that it is desirable to know ten times as much about a subject as you are actually going to use. It's a good principle since, although you may only use ten per cent of what you know, you never know *which* ten per cent you're going to need ahead of time.

There are two logical astronomical cycles that we can consider and which provide a broad basis for the astrological symbolism. One is to take the structure of the solar system, going outward from the sun, as a basis for the meanings of the planets. In this cycle, the Earth, the asteroids and the newly discovered minor planet Chiron, play a part. The second approach is to take the logical progression of the signs, from Aries to Pisces. If we assume that the sign, its ruler and the corresponding house are the same principle operating at different levels, it is possible to devise a system of twelve basic principles that contains the meanings of all the factors.

There are some objections to doing this since the traditional meanings do not always correspond as closely as might be desired. For example, Capricorn and the 10th house are regarded as rather go-getting and success oriented while the ruler, Saturn, has the meanings of delay and obstruction. Again, Mars and Aries seem to fit well as both representing initiation and outgoing energy, but the traditional meanings of the 1st house of personality and physical appearance do not, at first sight, seem to correspond with the pattern.

However, among other things, we are here concerned with redefining astrology in a way which is appropriate to our own times. We need not be too concerned with the traditional meanings, provided that the scheme that we finish up with is capable of including the traditional meanings as special cases of a more general principle. So, I am suggesting a scheme of twelve basic principles which includes the planets and starts with Mars as the ruler of Aries. We shall also later look at the meanings of the planets only in terms of the structure of the solar system, starting with the sun. The two systems have the same basic meaning for the planets but offer slightly different perspectives on them.

For the purposes of looking at the twelve principles, I will also do something which is rather unusual in the current literature and consider the rulers of Scorpio, Aquarius and Pisces to be, respectively, Mars, Saturn and Jupiter. In practice I would regard Uranus, Neptune, and Pluto in the chart as supporting indications from Aquarius, Pisces and Scorpio, respectively. I shall later argue that Uranus, Neptune and Pluto operate in a completely different sphere. Their effects, in the space-time world, are felt as distortions of the true principles, and the planets themselves should not be regarded as having displaced the old rulers. They can, though, usefully be regarded as *associated* with the signs that they are usually said to co-rule. As Robert Hand points out in *Horoscope Symbols*, the fit between Uranus and Aquarius is not, in fact, all that good. Seemingly, the fit of Scorpio-Pluto and Pisces-Neptune is good, but when we look at the meanings of the trans-Saturnians in detail we shall see that the fit is not as good as it appears.

I draw a considerable distinction between the fine logic of the abstractions and the manifestations of them at the level of the personality where the whole thing becomes blurred and ill defined anyway. In practice, I would regard Sun aspecting Neptune as a reinforcement of Sun in Pisces and, similarly, Uranus and Pluto aspects as supporting indications from Aquarius and Scorpio.

Considering the sign, its ruler and the corresponding house as being the same principle operating at different levels, we can say that the sign represents a need, the planet the drive to satisfy the need and the house the experience of the circumstances related to the need in the physical world. This, of course, is definitely not the same as saying that the sign,

138 / ROY ALEXANDER

planet and house are all the same thing. It is rather that all three levels are held within a more abstract context.

A useful analogy is that we all have a background need for food. It is there all the time, whether we are aware of it or not. This can be compared with the sign. Hunger is the drive to satisfy the need and is analogous with the planet. The house is whatever experience to do with eating our hunger leads us into. If there is no food in the house or we are on a diet, the experience may be one of not eating. In practice, the houses of a chart often have to do with the absence of certain experiences—the experience is an issue *in some way*.

A slightly different way of looking at it, already mentioned in Chapter 5, is that the planets are like engines producing certain types of thrust. The signs that the planets are in are like the particular type of fuel that is available for the engine to run on and the houses are the results. Mars in Leo in the 10th means that for this person to act with initiative and self-assertion he must have available a good, rather dramatic sense of his own individuality and considerable support from others. The assertion will generally manifest in ways which affect his status and achievements within a group.

The second analogy is perhaps the more useful in practice. It lends itself more readily to the situation which is most often found in practical interpretation where the signs, planets and houses are usually split up instead of being aligned with each other. Also, it emphasizes more than the first that the action is with the planet. In constructing meanings for sign-planet-house combinations, the planet is always like the verb in a sentence. Mars in Libra in the 5th is not the same as Venus in Aries in the 5th, although these are both combination of principles 1, 5 and 7. The first example is concerned with the type of "fuel" that the person needs to act; the second tells us what he needs to love.

The twelve principles, together with the signs, houses and planets that constitute them are listed in Table 2.1.1. These twelve principles can be seen as a logical cycle for the growth of a human being or any other entity. *They are there anyway, whether we apply astrological language to them or not.* As Dane Rudhyar has said, the astrology is a kind of algebra that enables us to define and explore the workings of the twelve principles. This is a crucial point because it gets us off the old red herring argument about whether the planets, signs and houses *cause* things or *influence* us. They don't, any more than the letters E, m and c "cause" $E = mc^2$. Yet, just as we need the letters E, m and c and the concepts they stand for to understand some aspects of the physical world, so do we need the symbols of astrology to enable us to handle the general processes of living. Some of the controversies in astrology are more apparent than real and arise from confusing a language with the things it is being used

The Twelve Principles	The Signs	The Houses	The Planets
1 Action	♈	1	♂
2 Maintenance	♉	2	♀
3 Communication	♊	3	☿
4 Foundation	♋	4	☽
5 Power	♌	5	☉
6 Adjustment	♍	6	☿
7 Relationship	♎	7	♀
8 Sharing	♏	8	♂ (♇)
9 Expansion	♐	9	♃
10 Construction	♑	10	♄
11 Liberation	♒	11	♄ (♅)
12 Uniting	♓	12	♃ (♆)

Table 2.1.1.

to describe. Some of them, such as the problems of the"correct" house system, perhaps reflect a lack of adequate understanding of the language.

The cycle of the twelve principles breaks down into two divisions. There is the first phase of 1 to 6, inclusive, where the focus is primarily on self, and the second phase, 7 to 12, inclusive, where the focus is primarily on others.

As an example of how the twelve principles operate as a cycle, let us take the case of a person embarking on the study of astrology. We will suppose that he follows the study through to the point where his interest in it moves to another level.

First Phase: The impulse to do it, buying an elementary text or signing up for lectures or a course.

Second Phase: Getting a grip of the basics of the subject so that he has some knowledge or resources of his own.

Third Phase: Collecting more knowledge that would have made no sense without the basics by reading more widely and discussing the subject with others.

Fourth Phase: Assimilating and integrating his knowledge in such a way that it becomes a workable part of him and he can say "I am an astrologer."

Fifth Phase: Beginning to use his knowledge, doing charts for friends and looking for feedback on his work.

Sixth Phase: Adjusting and improving his technique as a result of the experiences of phase five.

Up to this point, although he has been increasingly concerned with the reactions of other people, the emphasis has mainly been on self-development.

Seventh Phase: Taking his (temporarily) perfected knowledge out into the world. Actively seeking formally defined client relationships.

Eighth Phase: Becoming involved in a truly committed interchange with his clients, where assisting them is of more importance than parading his knowledge.

Ninth Phase: Arising from this, an increasing grasp of the underlying laws and principles of what he is doing.

Tenth Phase: Being sufficiently established in what he is doing to be able to write and teach. Constructing an "establishment" about himself, however small.

Eleventh Phase: Beginning to see the limitations of his system, efficient for his purposes though it may be.

Twelfth Phase: Being able to see what he has accomplished so far as a whole and being willing to let go of whatever attitudes and beliefs he needs to let go of to move to another level.

Phases 11 and 12 may need a little elaboration, perhaps because we encounter them rather less than the others. As an example, suppose when he started that our astrologer was mainly interested in predictions and outer events rather than character and inner structures. In phase 11, he may begin to feel that this is limiting and to find a psychological approach more interesting. In that case, in phase 12, he will have to confront and let go of a lot of assumptions about the importance of predictions and outer events.

As I have said, this twelvefold cycle is best used in understanding the signs and houses at an abstract level. It is not, at least in my experience, particularly useful to try to apply it directly to chart interpretation. An exception to this is that it can be of value when dealing with houses. If we are looking at the 5th house, say, to see how the person handles the experience of putting power out into the world, it can be very useful to look at the 4th to see what kind of a foundation he has to come from and at the 6th to see how he handles criticism and the need for self-adjustment. For example, if he has Aries on the cusp of the 5th and a Mars-Jupiter conjunction in the 5th, one would deduce a powerfully expressive person. But if he has Pisces on the 4th, as will usually be the case, and Saturn in the house, the foundation from which he expresses power and creativity is somewhat shaky and he will not do it with the confidence which one might expect if one does not take the cyclic view.

We may further suppose that he has Taurus on the 6th and Sun in Taurus in the 6th, which will give him a rather stubborn and unyielding attitude to criticism. This person may very well come on in a powerful way but there will be much insecurity and bravado to it that looking at the 5th house alone would not indicate.

To fit the planets into the system of twelve principles, we need to recognize that they each operate in a positive, masculine way and a negative, feminine way. It may seem strange to think of such an essentially male planet as Mars having a feminine face but, as Eighth Principle, it does. The basic energy of Mars is desire, which can be expressed as independent action or deep sharing. Mercury is conceptualization, which can be outgoing communication or inward adjustment. Venus is love, which can be maintaining things or situations or relating to others. Jupiter is expansion, which can be mental growth or spiritual union. Saturn is the need for form or structure. This can be expressed as maintaining old structures or seeking new ones.

We have already set the trans-Saturnians aside as being something different, and we need to recognize that Sun and Moon also fall into a different category from the planets proper. The convenience of lumping them in with the others and referring to all of them as "planets" tends to obscure this difference. Astronomically, we know that they are not planets at all and, just visually, they are obviously different from the others by virtue of their greater apparent size and colour. This is something that the older astrologers seem to have been more keenly aware of than we tend to be today. They referred to the Sun and Moon as the "lights" to distinguish them from the others.

We can regard Sun as being always masculine and Moon as always feminine. Unlike the five traditional planets which can work in both modes, Sun and Moon need to be treated as a pair. If we take it that this pair is central to the entire scheme we can arrive at an arrangement of signs and rulers which forms a logical pattern, with alternating masculine and feminine. (See Fig. 2.1.1.) It will be noticed that this arrangement recapitulates the astronomical order of the planets.

♌	☉ ☽	♋
♍	☿	♊
♎	♀	♉
♏	♂	♈
♐	♃	♓
♑	♄	♒

Figure 2.1.1 Signs and rulers in their alternating feminine and masculine modes.

The twelve principles themselves can further be broken down into an interplay between the three modes of being—cardinal, fixed and mutable (or, creating, maintaining and destroying)—and the four elements or types of energy—fire, air, water and earth.

The meanings of the elements can be summarized as follows:

Fire: The ability to perceive directly the meaning behind situations or events, to grasp potentials and possibilities. Freshness, childlike trust and enthusiasm. Idealism, originality. High energy and activity. A sense of urgency.

Earth: Practicality, strong sense awareness, does not look beyond the immediate facts, concerned with details. Perseverance, tenacity, poor initiative, needs to be motivated by others or by circumstances. Reserve, inertia, tends to conform to what is expected.

Air: Ability to make connections between perceived facts. Makes value judgments indirectly as a result of considering the factors involved. Harmony, friendliness, sociability. Tends to be impersonal, uncommitted, unemotional.

Water: Concerned with grasping the wholeness of a situation or thing in a directly experiential way. Tends to identify emotionally with what is going on. Makes direct value judgments on the basis of whether what is being considered causes pleasure or pain. Deeply emotional, vulnerable, romantic, impressionable, easily influenced by surroundings. Wisdom, compassion.

It remains to provide a definition of the three qualities. What I would suggest is that cardinal draws energy directly from the unconscious, fixed stores and transforms it so that it is available for conscious use, and mutable uses it consciously and with full choice.

The analogy of an electrical accumulator is useful, though it should not be pushed too far. The cardinal signs are like the current that charges the accumulator. The fixed signs correspond to the accumulator's ability to hold the charge and be ready to release it. The mutable signs correspond to the flow of energy when the accumulator is connected to an appliance.

Cardinal, then, is an unconscious, unidirectional charging up of interest or intention. Fixed is the storing and consolidating of this creative intention; mutable is conscious, multidirectional functioning.

The analogy with the storage battery soon breaks down but it may be useful in dealing with this somewhat elusive concept. One obvious weakness is that it implies that the fixed signs are not expressive. We may overcome this difficulty by supposing that the electricity is visible—with a different color for each element. A laser beam of light enters the battery, which glows with the stored energy. The flow of electricity in the circuits of the machine connected to the battery produces complex patterns of light.

Usually the elements and qualities are considered only to apply to the signs of the zodiac but they can equally well be used to understand the twelve principles at every level, bearing in mind that signs, planets and houses operate differently.

We shall look at the twelve principles in detail and see how their meanings derive from the main cycles and from the subsidiary cycles of qualities and elements.

First Principle

*Aries, 1st house, Mars,
cardinal, fire, positive*

The first principle is fire energy being used in the cardinal mode. First principle is motivated to act in a compulsive, personal way by the perception of the inherent meanings and possibilities of experience. There is no other choice than action. The cardinal pressure plunges first principle into any experience that goes beyond a minimum threshold level of interest for him. By derivation, we have the usually recognized qualities of initiative, enthusiasm, assertiveness and, because action rather than consolidation is all important, lack of staying power. But the underlying abstraction behind those qualities is the unconscious need to experience himself by asserting himself. Only by making vigorous and aggressive contact with his environment can he experience himself as being real.

Aries is the need to lead, to be independent, courageous, pioneering, to prove oneself through action. Negatively, it can be tactless, pushy, inconsiderate, inclined to take needless risks for the sake of doing so. The energy is powerful but uncertain. There is much fear of falling back into nothingness.

Mars is desire (defining desire as emotion which leads to action). The positive, first principle Mars is direct, outgoing, spontaneous action. It should be noted that what one desires and feels compelled to go for is not necessarily the same thing as what is wanted and valued, which is Venus. This can be a major source of conflict in a chart.

The traditional meaning of Mars as physical sexual drive and Venus as emotional love helps to illustrate the point. A man may want (Venus) a stable home and a conventional family life, yet his desires (Mars) lead him into a series of love affairs which could be detrimental to what he wants. Or, it may work the other way around. What his Venus function may want is a series of wild love affairs, yet his Mars energies pull him in the direction of a comfortable home and a stable marriage. In either case he has a conflict on his hands. The condition of Mars in the chart, by sign and house placement and aspect, gives information about the person's desire energy. Note that a strong Mars does not, of itself, mean that desires are readily expressed and satisfied. If there are blocks elsewhere in the chart, it may simply show a very high level of frustration.

A good example of the Aries face of Mars is the sports champion, going from one challenge to another.

The 1st house is your experience of your identity in terms of the way in which you present yourself to the world. It is not a very conscious experience because the focus is on doing rather than being aware of doing. It is the experience of learning a way to be in the world that works for us with other people. The cusp of the 1st house is the Ascendant—in all but one or two little-used house systems—and so has an importance greater than that given to the other house cusps. Aspects to the Ascendant give information about how the person experiences his own immediate approach to life. The sign on the Ascendant, the condition of the ruler by sign, house and aspect, and planets in the 1st house, give further information.

Second Principle

Taurus, 2nd house, Venus, fixed, earth, negative

The second principle is earth energy being used in the fixed mode. Second principle is motivated to increase his sense of being by holding within himself facts, methods and sensory awareness. The fixed pressure holds him in a pattern of staying with experiences that are trusted and familiar. By derivation, we have the usual second principle qualities such as conservation, reliability, slowness and unwillingness to change; the underlying abstraction of these qualities is the need to experience himself by identifying with the environment and possessing it. He is only able to experience himself by possessing the things that he is aware of, whether these be material objects or ideas.

Taurus is the need to be firmly rooted, to have a sense of self-worth, security, awareness of one's own resources, both material and psychological. It is the need to be practical, down to earth, sensuous, to have tangible results. After the outrush of energy in Aries, consolidation takes place; instead of the focus of interest being on exploring many possibilities, it is on developing some limited options.

The drive in second principle is the negative, feminine side of Venus. The action of loving, setting a value on things, operates magnetically, drawing the valued objects and persons to oneself so as to augment one's sense of identity. The condition of Venus in the chart by sign, house and aspect gives information about the person's ability to be attractive and to keep what he attracts.

As with Mars, the fact that Venus in the chart may be strong and prominent does not of itself mean that there are no problems with being attractive. Other functions may interfere with an otherwise healthy power of attraction, either restricting it or overdoing it. The less desirable effects of a Taurus Venus can be overindulgence in food, sex and other sensual pleasures, or an excessive preoccupation with money.

A good example of the Taurus face of Venus is the art collector who surrounds himself with objects that are not only valuable but beautiful.

The 2nd house is the experience of having resources and supplies, material and psychological, that enable you to reach out to the world. It is the experience of self-worth, of being loved, of having one's basic needs met and having the confidence that they will continue to be met. Basically, it is the experience of ownership, and in the slightly elusive sense of owning oneself, being "one's own person" as well as that of simply having possessions. The sign on the 2nd house cusp and the condition of its ruler, by sign, house and aspect and any planets in it, gives information about the person's experience of ownership and self-worth.

Third Principle

Gemini, 3rd house, Mercury,
mutable, air, positive

The third principle is air energy being used in the mutable mode. Third principle is motivated to function personally in many ways by observing, making comparisons, collecting information, finding relationships between his experiences and creating an intellectual framework for his life. The mutable pressure is a conscious one, and third principle has a good deal of choice about where he will direct his interest, that is to say, the *unconscious* charge on any particular thing will be low. By derivation we have the usually recognized qualities of versatility, changeableness, inconsistency. The underlying abstraction is the need to experience his identity through knowing his environment. Also, third principle is more conscious of the environment itself than are first and second and is in a position to recognize it as potentially threatening. The need of third principle to know is partly motivated by the need to control; "control" here is not manipulation but rather is akin to the magical belief that if you know the name of something, you have power over it.

Gemini is the need to be flexible, curious, relatively uncommitted, to play with words and ideas. It is the need to communicate, which sometimes manifests as a variety of physical skills or physical restlessness and nervousness as well as, or instead of, a flow of words. It is the need to be able to explain things, to have logical, concrete reasons, to be a neutral observer rather than a committed and involved participant.

The drive in third principle is the positive, masculine face of Mercury. The basic energy of Mercury is to conceptualize, to learn in order to be able to do, so Mercury energy is as much involved with learning a physical skill as with purely mental exercise.

There is no direct judgment of good and bad with Mercury; the energy is neutral. Learning and doing will be differently emphasized for different people. The doing may consist of little more than talking about what has been learned, as with a lecturer. On the other hand, a man whose job consists of tightening the screws on a car door on an assembly line will be using very little learning for a lot of doing.

An example of the Gemini face of Mercury is the war correspondent uninvolved with either side and going wherever the story is.

The condition of Mercury in the chart by sign, house and aspect gives information about the person's ability to conceptualize and communicate, to learn and to apply his learning. Again, a strong Mercury does not automatically mean that all will be well in this area. Other factors, for example severe emotional conflict, may interfere with the expression of the Mercury energy.

The 3rd house is the experience of having concrete knowledge of the world, of having logical, rational explanations for things and being able to maintain a neutral attitude. Basically it is the experience of knowing, reacting and relating to and handling the immediate environment, without commitment to any particular set of results or way of being. The sign on the cusp of the 3rd house, the condition of its ruler, and any planets in it, will give information about how the person deals with this experience.

Fourth Principle

Cancer, 4th house, Moon,
cardinal, water, negative

Fourth principle is water energy being used in the cardinal mode. Fourth principle is motivated to act in a compulsive, personal way by his awareness of values and the experience of pleasure and pain as intense subjective reality. We are back again to an unconscious cardinal pressure. Fourth principle has no choice but to create a matrix of habit patterns to attempt to experience pleasure and avoid pain. With the experience of third principle behind him, he is highly aware of his environment and, by derivation, we have the usually recognized qualities of self-protection, nurturing, emotionalism, concern with holding on. The underlying abstraction is the need to experience himself as a cohesive being by assimilating some parts of his environment and discarding others. He is caught between the cardinal pressure to gain more experience so as to build a more secure matrix of personality and the fear of encountering pain by doing so.

Cancer is the need for emotional security, warm and nurturing human relationships, to have the assurance of privacy and inviolable personal boundaries. The need often manifests as moodiness, extreme emotional vulnerability and very strong qualities of imagination and sensitivity. There is often possessiveness and a tendency to feel and act injured at the slightest hint of criticism. Essentially it is the need to live in a safe, protected cocoon, while at the same time relating to and dealing with the outer world. The two aims are not really compatible, hence the duality and inner split associated with Cancer.

The drive in fourth principle is the Moon. The Moon is always feminine, negative and does not have a masculine aspect. It is the drive to create a safe support system for oneself, both psychologically and materially, to create a flexible but automatic pattern of thought, feeling and action. Feeling is the major component. Thinking and doing have to be integrated into the feeling response. Clear, detached thinking is not a function of the Moon level. Nevertheless, decisions are made by the Moon function and it is the function which is primarily concerned with the formation of the script, discussed in Chapter 3, Part I.

The condition of the Moon in the chart, by sign, house and aspect, gives information about the way the person uses the drive to create a safe, protected space. Usually the Moon function is automatic and overdone. In terms of a growth-oriented astrology the Moon usually has a negative (in the sense of undesirable) connotation, since it indicates a holding on to the past.

An example of the Moon is a mother totally but unconsciously devoted to her children with no interests outside the home, and with the same attitudes to life and ways of doing things as *her* mother.

The 4th house is the experience of having a secure base from which to operate in the world. It is the experience of power which derives from internal and external security and acceptance. The sign on the 4th house and the condition of its ruler by sign, house and aspect, give information on the way the person experiences this private, personal power and security.

Fifth Principle

Leo, 5th house, Sun,
fixed, fire, positive

The fifth principle is fire energy being used in the fixed mode. Fifth principle is motivated to increase his sense of being by holding within himself his perception of meanings and the potentialities of his environment. We must note that the environment in fifth principle is very much larger than that in first, by virtue of the experience of second, third and fourth. The fixed pressure holds fifth principle in a pattern of high excitement in relation to the environment. By derivation we have the usually recognized qualities of self-expression, strong sense of ego, creativity, drama—in short, those qualities that tend to actualize the potential magnificence of which fifth principle is so strongly aware. The underlying abstraction is the need to experience himself by stamping the environment with his personality and having the environment reflect him. It would be a mistake to regard this as narcissism. It is not that fifth principle is in love with himself to the exclusion of others. The key concept is that of "feedback." He can only experience himself by getting his environment to respond to him.

Leo is the need to be acknowledged as something special and magnificent, to be self-assured, benevolent, confident. It is the need for dramatic and wholehearted self-expression. It has been compared to the orgasm, a total commitment of self-expressive and loving energy (ideally, that is.) The need often manifests as pride and willpower, with a great deal of unrealistic idealism.

The drive in fifth principle is the Sun, which is always masculine, positive and does not have a feminine aspect. The Sun is the drive to express the central will or purpose of the life; the drive for full expression as an individual human being; the full actualization of one's potential. From the point of view of a growth-oriented astrology the Sun can usually be regarded as a positive factor (in the sense of being desirable) since it is the drive to be released from and to transcend the past.

The condition of the Sun, by sign, house and aspect, gives information on how the person uses the drive for self-expression. Even if it is favorably placed and well aspected, this does not automatically mean that self-expression will be easy and fulfilling. In particular, the compulsive habit patterns of the Moon may militate against the healthy operation of the Sun drive.

An example of the Sun is a benevolent king taking a personal interest in the well-being of his subjects and his kingdom.

The 5th house is the experience of total personal self-expression, of individual creation or playfulness. Traditionally, children are allocated to the fifth house—a tangible result of the expression of creative energy. Essentially it is the experience of using the power generated in the privacy of the 4th house. The sign on the cusp of the 5th, the condition of its ruler, by sign, house position and aspects, and any planets in the house, show how the person relates to having this creative personal power available to him.

Sixth Principle

Virgo, 6th House, Mercury,
mutable, earth, negative

The sixth principle is earth energy being used in the mutable mode. Sixth principle is motivated to function personally in many ways and with conscious awareness in order to handle sense data, to make use of facts, methods and techniques and to operate efficiently in relation to others. Sixth principle has conscious use of the material that second principle could only unconsciously identify with. He is highly aware of how he can affect his environment and how it is likely to respond to him—having discovered this in the fifth principle stage. The need to know and learn in order to control is now applied in concrete terms. It is not enough, as it was in third principle, merely to know the magical name. Sixth principle has to come to terms with the physical reality of his environment and order it. By derivation we have the usually recognized qualities of industry, analysis, criticism and practicality. The underlying abstraction is the need to experience himself as skilled in relating to and managing his environment.

Virgo is the need for techniques for self-expression, for control of the emotions. It is the need to be self-analytical, discriminating, modest, to play down one's individuality in deference to others. In the Leo phase the creative energy is expressed in order to excite the admiration of others; this admiration is not always forthcoming and adjustments have to be made to the performance. The need often manifests as a tendency to be finicky and perfectionist, expecting perfection of oneself and of other people too. The critical faculty of Virgo may indeed turn to a very critical attitude to other people, whether this is openly expressed or not.

The drive in the sixth principle is the feminine, negative face of Mercury, the basic nature of which was discussed under third principle. Here, the drive to learn in order to do, to conceptualize in order to handle the world, is turned inward. Negative Mercury is more concerned with value judgments—though on the basis of intellectual assumptions or on the basis of results. Thus, Mercury will judge certain feelings and actions as good or bad because they produce desirable or undesirable results—as distinct from Venus, which judges good or bad as inherent qualities. Mercury can be assumed to operate through both faces in a chart, and the chart as a whole will give indications whether the positive or negative face is likely to be predominant. For instance, if Mercury is in a positive sign or house, it will tend to favor the Gemini expression; in a negative sign or house, the Virgo expression. This will be especially so, of course, if Mercury is actually in Gemini or Virgo.

An example of negative Mercury is the scientist at work in the laboratory intent on discovering processes that get the results he wants.

The 6th house is the experience of having techniques that work, of feeling well adjusted and useful in the world. The basic experience is that of personal growth. Traditionally the 6th house is related to health, and ill health can be regarded as the growth process dramatizing the fact that change and adjustment are needed. The sign on the cusp of the 6th house and the condition of its ruler by sign, house and aspects, and any planets in the house, show how the person relates to the experience of personal growth and adjustment.

As we have progressed through the first six principles the emphasis has gradually been shifting from self to others. In first principle, other people hardly count at all except as they present challenges. They become increasingly important as suppliers of stability, information, support, admiration and, finally, criticism, but even in the sixth principle the balance of interest is on the self. As we go through the next six principles, the balance of attention and interest shifts to others, starting with seventh principle when others become of equal importance for the first time.

Seventh Principle

Libra, 7th house, Venus,
cardinal, air, positive

The seventh principle is air energy being used in the cardinal mode. Seventh principle is motivated to relate to others in a compulsive way by observing, comparing and mentally creating a social framework in which deficiencies can be supplied by others. The cardinal, unconscious pressure is operative again, and seventh principle has no choice but to move outward to experience others as beings in their own right. He needs to find out about them and experiment with ways of relating. By derivation, we have the usually recognized seventh principle qualities of sociability, liking for harmony, low emotional commitment. The underlying abstraction is the need to experience himself *and* the environment simultaneously and as of equal importance. Satisfying this need is easier if the environment is pleasant—hence the need for harmony with companions and surroundings. Hence, too, the manifestation of a liking for various art forms, since art is a way of arranging at least a small part of the environment so that it is harmonious and "right."

Libra is the need for equal cooperative relationships, without dependency, both partners contributing as beings who are choosing to share. It is the need to relate from a position of strength yet with the recognition that true completeness is only possible in the context of a relationship. The concern for getting it right and so maintaining harmony and balance frequently manifests as no action or decision being taken at all or being left to others. Also, the need for equality means that Libra is somewhat afraid of deep feeling, unless he can be sure that it will be reciprocated.

The drive in seventh principle is the masculine, positive face of Venus. In contrast to the attracting mode of operation of the Taurus Venus, the act of loving and valuing is projected outward. Ultimately, the ability to love another person depends on our ability to love ourselves, so the functioning on the Libra Venus implies enough spare self-esteem (2nd principle) to be projected out onto the world.

The condition of Venus in the chart shows the person's ability for projecting love in equal relationships and whether it is likely to manifest more as positive or negative Venus.

An example of positive Venus is the diplomat, seeking equal and fair relationships, using skill to create harmony.

The 7th house is the experience of having equal relationships and finding self-fulfillment through being receptive to the needs of another or others. The sign on the cusp, the condition of its ruler, and any planets in the house will show how the person relates to this experience.

Eighth Principle

Scorpio, 8th house, Mars/Pluto,
fixed, water, negative

The eighth principle is water energy being used in the fixed mode. Eighth principle is motivated to increase his sense of being in relation to others by holding within himself his awareness of values and experience of pleasure and pain as intense, subjective reality. The fixed state holds him in a high state of sensitivity. In fourth principle, under the cardinal pressure, water energy has an escape mechanism if feelings become too much because the cardinal mode can shift to another point of interest. Eighth principle has to stay and take it, no matter how heavy the going is. By derivation, we have the usually recognized qualities of intensity, control, endurance, vengefulness. The underlying abstraction is the need to identify with the environment while staying conscious of his own identity. By fulfilling other's needs as though they were his own, eighth principle satisfies his own needs. If this is to be at all successful there has to be a powerful purging of the personality and, indeed, a "death" of such parts of the personality as hinder this need. From this point of view the underlying meaning of the association with death, elimination and sexualtiy is clear.

Scorpio is the need for intense, deeply involved and committed emotional relationships, and the need also for secrecy and privacy about such relationships to protect one's hidden power and sensitivity. It is the need to be passionate, penetrating, to seek the truth even when it is painful, to be powerful and self-controlled. It is the need to choose between identifying with emotions in order to wallow in them or in order to transcend them. The need often manifests as taciturnity, with excessive surface control inhibiting the emotional flow so that much of the energy is brooding and inward.

The drive in eighth principle is the feminine, negative face of Mars. Mars as desire energy has been discussed under first principle. In its negative polarity, desire is just as strong but is much more deliberate and considered. Where first principle Aries desire is a spontaneous searching out for what is desired, negative Mars desire operates through planning, seemingly cold and sometimes ruthless. Always the reactions of others, actual and likely, are involved in the attainment of one's own desire.

The condition of Mars in the chart shows how desire will operate and whether the Mars energy is likely to be used predominantly in the positive or negative mode.

An example of negative Mars is the politician calculating advantages and consequences and setting in motion a complex series of events to get what he secretly wants.

Pluto is also generally considered to be associated with the eighth principle, and its house position and aspects should be considered in evaluating eighth principle in the chart. The meaning of Pluto will be discussed more fully in the next section.

The eighth house is the experience of having intense, committed relationships that are a source of emotional power and an opportunity for growth. The sign on the cusp, the condition of its ruler and any planets in this house show how the person relates to the experience of deep commitment.

Ninth Principle

Sagittarius, 9th house, Jupiter,
mutable, fire, positive

The ninth principle is fire energy being used in the mutable mode. Ninth principle is motivated to function in many ways in relation to others by his perception of potentials and inherent meanings. We have again the fire excitement that we encountered in first and fifth principle, but now it is far more consciously expressed and the environment in which it functions is far wider. After the experience of eighth principle, ninth has an intuitive knowledge of others and is eager to organize and use this knowledge of the inner meaning of social relationships. By derivation, we have the usually recognized qualities of enthusiasm, frankness, friendliness, optimism. Ninth principle is often described as "freedom-loving," but this is a little misleading. It is true as far as it goes, but the kind of freedom involved is the sort that goes with being an accepted member of the community. In ninth principle, the sense of separate individuality has begun to sink very low. The underlying abstraction is the need for a total experience of the environment. Third principle sought to control the environment by knowing it. Ninth principle seeks to yield to the environment by allowing it to know him.

Sagittarius is the need for expansion, to have broad, philosophical viewpoints and understanding of life. It is the need to "know why" rather than "know how," the need for workable principles and ethical and moral judgments. The need can often manifest as impersonal attitudes and intolerance. The search for one's place in a greater whole is urgent in Sagittarius and can overshadow more directly personal interests. This can lead to fanatacism and zealous defending what Sagittarians perceive to be the truth. At the least, tact and subtlety are not usually highly regarded.

The drive in ninth principle is the positive face of Jupiter. This is the first time we have encountered a planetary drive that is more concerned with society at large than with the individual personality. Jupiter is the drive to expand, to acquire social esteem and value. In its positive mode it has characteristics of an explorer even though the exploring may be inward rather than physical. Key functions of Jupiter are assimilation and cooperation and also to protect what has been gained—thus the traditional link with financial and legal matters. Jupiter is also the drive to believe and have faith, since in order to expand one must have the faith that it is possible to do so.

An example of Sagittarius Jupiter is the explorer, motivated by a passionate belief in himself and his quest, pushing back the boundaries of knowledge.

The placement of Jupiter in the chart by sign, house and aspect gives information on how the person uses his expansion drive and whether it is most likely to operate in the Sagittarius or Pisces mode.

The ninth house is the experience of having convictions which expand and improve oneself, of exchanging and disseminating ideas through publishing, traveling and similar expansive activities. The sign on the house cusp, the condition of the ruler and any planets in the house will show how the person relates to this experience.

Tenth Principle

Capricorn, 10th house, Saturn,
cardinal, earth, negative

The tenth principle is earth energy operating in the cardinal mode. Tenth principle is motivated to act in relation to others in a compulsive way by his awareness of facts, sense data, practical needs and problems. Again, we are dealing with unconscious, cardinal pressure. Tenth principle is compelled to take the knowledge gained by ninth principle and organize it into a rigid, stable framework. The underlying abstraction is the need to experience the environment as defining oneself totally. Fourth principle was environmental stimuli used to create a personality matrix. Tenth principle fits himself into the existing matrix of the environment, and in tenth principle the sense of individuality is at its lowest ebb. The unit exists only to serve the purposes of the whole.

Capricorn is the need for stable and continuing respect and recognition from others by virtue of one's achievements and position. It is the need to be ambitious, practical and resourceful, to have recognized responsibilities, to be honorable and trustworthy. The main focus of interest in Capricorn is on form and correctness. There is a great need for a sense of socially acceptable purpose to the life. The need often manifests as perseverance, thrift, being businesslike and industrious.

The drive in tenth principle is the negative face of Saturn. Again, we are dealing with a planet whose main focus is social rather than personal. Saturn essentially is the drive to give concrete form to things, to set boundaries and concentrate power within established limits. The negative Capricorn face of Saturn is concerned primarily with establishing these boundaries and working within them. Hence, this mode of Saturn is felt often as restriction and inhibition. Negative Capricorn Saturn is the drive to establish a social identity by conforming to the rules and requirements of our particular group.

The demands of Saturn will vary from culture to culture and from one historical period to another. The requirements for gaining respect and recognition from our society are different now from what they were in Victorian times. They are different in civilized societies from what they are in some primitive societies where stealing and killing are regarded as valuable social attributes. The placement of Saturn in the chart, by sign, house, and aspect gives information on the way the person uses the drive for limitation and whether it will operate primarily in the Capricorn or Aquarius mode.

An example of Capricorn Saturn is a civil servant, recognized for his power and position, and operating through clearly defined processes and within definite limits.

The 10th house is the experience of having a clearly defined place within the group; the experience of guaranteed protection and acceptance, as long as the individual stays within his allotted place. The sign on the cusp and the condition of its ruler and any planets in the house show how the person relates to the experience of having social identity.

Eleventh Principle

Aquarius, 11th house, Saturn/Uranus,
fixed, air, positive

The eleventh principle is air energy operating in the fixed mode. Eleventh principle is motivated to increase his sense of being in relation to others by observing, comparing, reasoning. He is dealing with the same material as third and seventh principles but, unlike them, he is forced to do something with the material as the fixed pressure holds him to a definite focus. Eleventh principle is concerned with the power of ideas and especially the power of ideas to create new social realities. It is to do with the power of ideas to create a group consciousness and purpose and, as fifth principle was the free expression of personal identity, so is the eleventh principle the expression of a group identity. Fifth principle means stepping out of the matrix of *personal* identity in order to express the power inherent in it and eleventh principle means stepping out of the matrix of *social* identity to express the power inherent in it. By derivation we have the usually recognized qualities of originality, rebelliousness, humanitarianism. The underlying abstraction is the need to experience oneself operating powerfully and creatively in unison with others. There is still little sense of individual being. Eleventh principle thinks in terms of humanity, not of individual men and women. He is concerned with the rights of the individual, but only in an abstract way.

Aquarius is the need to break up old structures in order to create new ones. As we saw, Capricorn is concerned with power created by structure, but with the emphasis on using the power to maintain the structure. In Aquarius the need is to use structure in order to release power. It is the need to do things differently, to be original, rebellious, independent. But the independence is relative. The need is really to break down limits that have become oppressive so that a new group awareness can emerge.

The drive in eleventh principle is the positive face of Saturn. As we have seen, this is the drive to release power that has been created by social structures, the power that is available by virtue of an established social position. The placing of Saturn in the chart by sign, house position and aspect will give information on how the person uses the drive to create new realities, and whether Saturn is likely to operate most in the positive or negative mode.

Uranus is also associated with eleventh principle and must be examined but will be dealt with in a separate section.

An example of Aquarius Saturn is the revolutionary, working out and implementing new social realities and motivated by his perception that the existing power structures have become life denying. The 11th house is the experience of being involved with others for a common purpose. The sign on the cusp and the condition of the ruler by sign, house and aspect and any planets in the house show how the person handles this experience.

Twelfth Principle

Pisces, 12th house, Jupiter/Neptune,
mutable, water, negative

The twelfth principle is water energy operating in the mutable mode. Twelfth principle is motivated to function in many ways in relation to others by his perception of values and wholeness and the experience of pleasure and pain as intense subjective reality. Under the pressure of mutable energy, twelfth principle has the unconditional freedom to experience everything. By derivation, we have the usually recognized qualities of vagueness, transcendence, impressionability, elusiveness. The underlying abstraction is the need to experience the self as being at one with the environment—and, in this case, we may define the environment as being the universe. The difference between this and the state of affairs in tenth and eleventh principle may need some expansion. Tenth principle allows the group to define him, but only those parts of the group that are seen as being "correct." Eleventh principle needs group power but, again, it is the power of like-mindedness. Twelfth principle embraces the entire group, whether it is in agreement with the self or not. It is the end of a cycle and therefore contains the potential of another cycle.

Pisces is the need for transcendent, infinite love and beauty, the need for inner strength, faith in the unknown. It is the need to be imaginative, idealistic, self-expressive. Since it is the need to embrace everything, it is nonselective and everything is as important as everything else. There can therefore be a strong attachment to potential, a reluctance to manifest in concrete form, which may operate as a low commitment to the outer world with a high commitment to inner values. Self-confidence in dealing with the world is not high.

The drive in twelfth principle is negative Jupiter. As we have seen, Jupiter is expansion. In ninth principle the expansion occurs as an outward thrust. In twelfth principle it is more as though the experience rushes in as if to fill a vacuum. Negative Jupiter expands by becoming rather than by conquering. With negative Jupiter the functions of faith and belief operate in terms of having faith that God or the universe will be supportive; it is a passive rather than an active belief.

The placing of Jupiter in the chart will give information on the way the passive expansion drive works, and whether Jupiter's action is likely to be predominantly positive or negative.

Neptune is also associated with the twelfth principle and its placing must be considered. It will be dealt with in a separate section.

An example of negative Jupiter is the creative artist, or writer, allowing himself to be taken over by the energy of his inner perceptions.

The 12th house is the experience of confronting oneness with the universe or, in terms of the first three chapters of this book, of confronting one's responsibility for having created it. In practice, this means confronting, and letting go of, script patterns, and the 12th house is, correctly, associated with self-inflicted pain and suffering and behavior that seems self-destructive. Ultimately it is the experience of one's true power. The sign on the cusp of the house, the condition of its ruler and any planets in the house show how the person approaches this experience.

2

Planets

The meanings of the planets have been discussed in the previous chapter but, for greater understanding of them, it is helpful to look at them separately. This is particularly so for Uranus, Neptune and Pluto. These are frequently stated to be "higher octaves" of Mercury, Venus and Mars, respectively, and that they have now taken over the rulerships of Aquarius, Pisces and Scorpio, respectively, but usually without any very clear examination of the issues. As a matter of fact, it is very difficult to grasp the meanings of Uranus, Neptune and Pluto with the rational mind, but we can approach a sense of what they are about. First, let us divide the planets into four groups:

1. Sun, Moon
2. (Sun), Mercury, Venus, Mars, asteroids, Jupiter, Saturn
3. Chiron
4. Uranus, Neptune, Pluto

This is the first mention of the planet Chiron or of the asteroids in this book. Chiron was discovered in 1977 and is a very small planet that orbits between Saturn and Uranus. Not very much is known about it yet, but it does seem to act as a definite link between groups 3 and 4. I have not included it in the twelve principles, though it may be connected with seventh principle. At the time of writing I am not sufficiently clear about how it works in individual charts to know how to use it. Nevertheless it needs to be mentioned for the sake of completeness and we will see later how it fits into the planetary sequence.

The asteroid belt is included because it has significance in understanding the planetary cycle. I do not, in practice, use asteroids in interpretation, though ephemerides of some of the larger ones are available.

The planetary sequence is basically the same one described in the introduction to the 12 principles and is the astronomical one. For greater clarity, we need to consider it as two systems, one consisting of Sun and Moon, the other consisting of Sun and the rest of the true planets.

Sun and Moon

The Sun is the central will to live. It is not organic, psychological life as we understand it but, rather, the potential of life. It is purpose, defining purpose as a continuing drive to manifest one's being. It has the meaning of "wanting to." The Sun in the chart shows how we express our central purpose, how we strive to align all the disparate elements of the chart with the purpose of our individual Sun.

The Moon is the matrix of physical and emotional structures that brings this all "down to earth" and enables the potential to become actual. It is the basic stimulus-response survival mechanism that modifies the unwavering purpose of the Sun and adapts it to a form suitable for physical plane expression.

Let us take the analogy of a fairly complex piece of electrical equipment, say a tape recorder. Without a battery in it, the tape recorder is useless. The recorder here corresponds to the Moon. The battery may be compared with the Sun; it is potential energy, a central source of power. By itself it is no guarantee of whether or how the tape recorder will work and by itself, it is of no practical use. If it is fitted into a tape recorder that is in good working order, the machine becomes alive and can be used in a wide variety of ways.

An even better analogy for the Sun-Moon level of being is a computer. The computer will respond intelligently to anything it is programmed to deal with. A human being operating at this level is functioning only in the foundations of life. There is little scope for personal growth, though, of course, the lunar structures may be very complex and rich in themselves. In practice you won't find anyone who operates only at the Sun-Moon level, though very primitive communities would be pretty close to doing so. An amusing fictional example of someone operating at this level is P.G. Wodehouse's Lord Emsworth, the dreamy backwoods peer whose main interests in life are his prize pig and being left in peace. This is not to say, of course, that someone operating at the Sun-Moon level would necessarily be withdrawn and dreamy. He might be very intrusive and aggressive if that is his programming. One thinks of the sort of characters often played by Anthony Quinn.

The Sun-Moon functions are operating all the time, even when we are asleep. Body, feeling and mind processes go on although we may not be aware of them except through the medium of dreams. It may be said that the Sun-Moon pairing is what we share with all sentient life. The lunar structures of a man are vastly more complex than those of a caterpillar, and those of a cat will be somewhere in between. Nevertheless, the principle is the same—the will to life expressing through conscious and unconscious structures which are based on feeling responses.

The Sun-Moon pair can be said to be a basic mode of being, a permanent background coloring of our lives.

Mercury to Saturn

These are the planets of what Dane Rudhyar calls organic living. In other words, they are functions which we all use in our daily lives. There is a greater degree of choice about the extent to which we use these planets, and situations can arise in which we are almost totally functioning in one planet. A man in the heat of battle (Mars) is not likely to be making much use of his reasoning and perceptive powers (Mercury). It is true that he may be planning some strategy as he fights, but this is going to be based on previous training or experience or perhaps just mental rehearsal of what he would do in these circumstances. Whatever thinking he is doing should more properly be referred to the ever-active Moon function, certainly if he is in a berserk rage.

The Sun-planets system is a much more complex one than the Sun-Moon system. The planets can be thought of as a logical sequence whose meaning depends on their relationship to the Sun and the Earth.

Exactly what the Earth means in astrology is usually evaded. If it is dealt with at all it is usually described as "yourself," though it is not made clear what this "self" is in relation to the various planetary functions. The point is not an easy one. As always, when trying to describe psychological processes, we are dealing with elusive concepts that, by their nature, can only be partially grasped by the concrete, reasoning mind. Astronomically, one thing is clear and that is that the Earth is the standpoint from which the planets, signs and houses are viewed. Psychologically, then, it should be the standpoint from which "you" view your drives, needs and goals. It is that place of detachment, of pure consciousness and will, from which we realize that we *have* drives, needs and goals and that we are not those drives, needs and goals. It is a place within ourselves which is rarely attained, except by special meditation exercises, and, even then, the sense of the disidentified "I" is likely to be fleeting. The "I" is normally caught up with and identified with some other part of the personality. Possibly this is why the meaning of the Earth astrologically has had so little attention. Unless we make a special effort, we are not usually aware of it.

The planets should perhaps not be thought of as functions in themselves but, rather, as differentiations of the primary solar will to life, in the same way as the colors of the spectrum are a differentiation of white light.

Before anything can come into physical manifestation, it must first be an idea, a mental construct, and the first differentiation of the Sun's purpose is Mercury, the principle of mental activity. By itself, an idea will not manifest. It needs to be given value and charged with feeling and magnetism, so the second differentiation is Venus. Next, some action has to be taken to bring the idea into manifestation. This is the Mars function. Note that Mars is the first planet beyond the orbit of the Earth and is the first planetary principle that expresses as outer action.

Beyond Mars lie the asteroids, which are not normally considered in astrology. However, they have their place in the psychological sequence because Mars action is always disruptive inasmuch as it breaks up existing conditions and changes them. The asteroids may be thought of as the debris of the old patterns which Mars has broken up. It may be that the effort of dealing with the debris is too great and the Mars will fails, in which case the sequence is aborted. Mars is acting as personal will, which is a substitute for the solar will and may or may not be in line with it.

Jupiter, the function of faith, optimism and social purpose, is on the other side of the asteroid belt. If the Mars energy can be sustained by the confidence and perception of a larger meaning and framework of Jupiter, it can go through the obstacles represented by the asteroids, gaining value (Jupiter) as it does so, and finally manifesting in some concrete and clearly defined form in Saturn.

Let us apply this sequence to a specific example to make it clearer. Suppose we have a man who is working in a routine and unsatisfying job. One day he gets the idea (Mercury) that he could have his own business. This may remain no more than an idea for some time but eventually he develops a charge of excitement and feeling about it (Venus). This builds up into a strong desire (Mars) and he leaves his job and sets up for himself (Mars).

At this point he is going to encounter some difficulties which he may or may not have foreseen (asteroids). His income may drop, creating family difficulties; he has to address himself to the different set of problems attendant on being self-employed. If, however, his perception of the value and meaning of what he is doing is strong enough (Jupiter), he will overcome these problems and increase his available energy for his project in doing so. He will be able to establish himself (Saturn) as a businessman in his own right.

The sequence is the outward flow of solar energy, but there is an inward flow as well. Grounded in the permanent structures of Saturn, the energy can perceive the possibilities of further expansion (Jupiter). This time the obstacles (asteroids) can be tackled at greater leisure and with existing optimism. If the Jupiter function has not run to extravagance, the asteroid obstacles can be planned for in advance. Action is then taken (Mars), resulting, if all goes well, in an increase of self-worth (Venus). The magnetizing effect of increased self-worth gives rise to an increased capacity for ideas, thinking and communicating (Mercury). Coming back to our example, the established businessman, confident of his position (Saturn), may decide to expand by producing another line of goods in addition to his existing one (Jupiter). At this point he may be so carried away by the optimism of Jupiter that he does not take proper account of the difficulties that he will have to overcome (asteroids). In this case he is in for trouble. If, however, he plans wisely (Jupiter) and takes a realistic account of his limitations (Saturn), all should be well. He then goes into the new line of business (Mars). If it is successful, his estimate (Venus) of himself as a businessman is increased. This spurs him to get more ideas for his business and probably brings him more business contacts (Mercury).

So the solar purpose, or the purpose of the Self, has been accomplished not only by the outward flow but also by the inward flow. Even if there is a failure at some point in the sequence, something has still been accomplished, and it cannot be stressed too much that what may be experienced as pain or failure by the personality may be a success from the point of view of the Self, or the total psyche.

Although the planetary functions have been described as a logical sequence, and should be regarded as such, in practice they can, and do, operate out of sequence. Also, there is usually a two-way flow between consecutive planets before the next stage is achieved. The man's first idea of his own business is Mercury. Getting strong feelings about it is Venus. He will then have to go back to Mercury to do some more thinking which will further stimulate the excitement (Venus). In the same way, we saw that, on the return flow, it was necessary for the optimism of Jupiter to refer back to the practical limitation and support of Saturn.

Perhaps the most frequent example of a function acting out of sequence is Saturn in his aspect of fear and pessimism. This can come in and kill the whole thing at the Mercury stage. Or perhaps the man will get to the point of being ready to act and stops himself by allowing Saturn to come in prematurely. Or, with a man of different temperament, Jupiter may move in too fast and generate action based on unrealistic optimism.

Uranus, Neptune and Pluto

Although the sequence Mercury through Saturn has much greater possibilities of growth than Sun-Moon, it is still something that takes place in the space-time-energy universe. In order to do anything in the Mercury through Saturn sequence it is necessary to establish a process, a linear sequence of events. This is what we do in the course of ordinary, organic living, where it is necessary to accomplish things in the physical world.

There is, however, another space which is beyond words where all we have to do to accomplish something is to create it by declaring that it is so. Perhaps it is more accurate to say that we create it by being willing to have it be so. Thus, if I say "Everything in my life, no matter how seemingly bad or restricting, is an opportunity for growth," then that is so simply by virtue of my creating it that way. I don't have to go through any process to arrive at the result. I don't have to prove it to anybody. What I have done is to create a context in which the events in my life, good or bad, pleasant or unpleasant, are opportunities for growth. Or, I may say, "Whatever happens in our relationship, no matter how tacky and distorted it gets, is an expression of my total love for you." Instantly that is so and there is a point at which it is crystal-clear obvious, though one does not arrive at this by any process of understanding. It is like getting the point of a joke or experiencing a poetic image.

This is Uranus, the magician. Werner Erhard calls this act of instant creation "the magic wand." With the repeated caution that words cannot do more than point toward the meaning of the trans-Saturnian planets, we may say that Uranus is liberation from the time-and-space-bound processes of the planets which are enclosed by the orbit of Saturn. For the most part, we are very hypnotized by the seeming reality of the space-time universe and the linear processes of the intra-Saturnian planets so that we ordinarily pay little attention to the existence of this faculty. To borrow another image from Werner Erhard, it is like having an automobile sitting outside the house; we have the keys to it but we hardly ever put the keys in the ignition and go for a drive.

This is not to say that we never use the energy of Uranus, just that few of us do it consciously or frequently. So, very often, the Uranus energy operates as some kind of disruption of the intra-Saturnian functions—an accident, a sudden and unexpected piece of good luck, insights, unusual viewpoints. If the energy is very powerful and very blocked, it will work out as eccentricity, rebelliousness. It can be seen to be an extension of the eleventh principle.

So, Uranus is making the jump to a level of consciousness that is not space-time bound. But making the jump is not the end of the matter. The act of creating the new context, the insight, has to be manifested in the space-time world. The first reaction of the space-time consciousness is to invalidate the new context. The day after I choose to create the context of "everything that happens in our relationship is an expression of my total love for you," I find myself hating you. I discover faults I've never seen before. You are a source of anger and irritation for me. There comes a stage of being willing to come from the new context no matter what. No matter how stupid it looks to say that my hatred for you is an expression of my total love for you, I continue to operate from that context. It doesn't mean I stop hating you or I pretend it doesn't matter. It means I *include* hating you in ultimately loving you. This is the Neptune function. Neptune is the ability to include everything and also to dissolve the rigid structures and habit patterns of Saturn.

Again, we don't usually use it in the way I have described, and the more usual manifestations of Neptune are far less conscious. It often operates as confusion and illusion. *Pretending* I don't hate you when I do and that everything is somehow dreamy and romantic is unconscious Neptune. Neptune in a chart can often productively be interpreted as an attachment to potential or formlessness, a reluctance to take concrete form. It is still the same energy of boundlessness and all-inclusion, and is clearly an extension of the 12th principle.

Finally (it is impossible not to use words that imply a linear sequence), the whole of my life becomes permeated by the new context. My entire relationship with you in its most mundane details is aligned with the context of my total love for you. The content of the relationship is sort of ground up, put through a different mill by the new context. Everything in the relationship becomes a manifestation of my total love for you. The relationship is renewed, purged of petty neurotic games playing and absolutely transformed.

This is the action of Pluto and I would like to quote Dane Rudhyar's definition of Pluto from *The Practice of Astrology:*

> Pluto produces a new pattern of integration with an insistence that tends to obliterate even the memory of the past, pulverizing the structures of old and cementing the remains into a screen upon which to project the new Image.*

*Reprinted by special arrangement with Shambhala Publications, Inc., 1920 13th Street, Boulder, Colorado 80302. From *The Practice of Astrology* © 1968 by Dane Rudhyar, p. 73.

From the point of view of interpreting a chart, Pluto is relentless, underground power tending to create unity. It can often manifest as obsession or ruthlessness. It can be seen to be an extension of eighth principle and therefore the co-ruler of Scorpio, but some astrologers have assigned it to Aries. Certainly the action of Pluto leads to a rebirth and a new beginning and is therefore appropriate to first principle and Aries. The point is interesting, but as far as practical chart interpretation is concerned, I would recommend that Pluto be regarded as associated with Scorpio and the natural 8th house.

Equally, in practical interpretation, Uranus and Neptune can be regarded as associated with Aquarius and Pisces, bearing in mind that they do not truly belong in the same realm as the intra-Saturnian planets. They can be looked to to see where the person might be encouraged to make the jump to a new context. For instance, the first example I used— "everything is an opportunity for growth"—might refer to Uranus in the 9th house or in aspect with Jupiter. The second example might be Uranus in the 7th or in aspect with Venus. It is not possible at this stage to offer more than hints here.

Many astrology texts take the position, by implication at least, that the trans-Saturnians have taken over from the old rulers. I would recommend that the old rulers continue to be used alongside the new associates.

Finally, there is the question of interpreting Uranus, Neptune and Pluto by sign. The most generally prevailing view about this seems to be that these planets stay so long in a sign that their effect is a very general one and should be ignored in the interpretation of an individual chart. On the whole I go along with this, and for the most part I would look at these three planets only by house and aspects. If Pluto in Cancer is the only planet in Cancer in the chart, I would not expect to see very much emphasis on the nurturing principle unless the 4th house is heavily tenanted. I think, though, that it is valuable to note that the person does have access to *some* Cancerian energy.

Chiron

It seemed best to leave this maverick until Uranus, Neptune and Pluto had been dealt with. The discovery of a new planet—making it public knowledge—seems to coincide with a much wider availability of the energy of that planet. Thus the tremendous scientific and technological advances of the last 200 years began around the time of the discovery of Uranus. The discovery of Neptune correlated with interest in the paranormal, the use of anesthetics and speculations about the nature of the mind. The discovery of Pluto coincided with the release of atomic energy.

Chiron seems to be a bridge between space-time bound conscious-ness and the "magic wand" consciousness, as its orbit, linking Saturn and Uranus, would suggest. In broad terms I suggest that its discovery means that the ability to make the kind of conscious jump that I have described is becoming more generally available. In terms of the individual chart it seems to act as an irritant. The affairs of the house it occupies and the energies of planets it aspects are kept off balance and goaded as if to remind one that the context-creating space is available—the automobile is out there waiting for us to drive it.

However, unless it makes a tight aspect (2 or 3 degrees) with Ascendant, MC, Sun, Moon, Mercury, Venus or Mars, it seems to remain a dumb note, and even when it does make such an aspect its effect often seems obscure. It certainly should be noted. My own personal practice at the time of writing is not to enter it in the chart but to list it on a separate sheet of paper with my other calculation notes.

Moon's Nodes

The nodes of the Moon are not planets, but it is convenient to consider them here. They are the points at which the Moon's orbit intersects the apparent path of the Sun and so are always exactly 180° apart. There is no widespread agreement on their meanings but there are two suggested meanings I have found to work for me.

The first is that they operate as a polarity, with the North Node showing, by its house position, the area of life where there is much opportunity for growth but where considerable effort is needed. The South Node, in the opposite house, shows an area in which the experiences come easily and naturally and which, in consequence, is likely to be used as an easy way out. One can say that the North Node's house shows the set of experiences, the mastery of which is a particular task for this incarnation; the South Node's house the experiences one will characteristically turn to as a way of avoiding that task.

Thus with North Node in 7th house and South Node in 1st, for example, relationships will be a rough ride but an area of enormous potential growth. However, relative ease of self-assertion and going one's own way enable the person to cop out fairly easily from the difficulties of relating. If the positions are reversed then the prime task will be self-assertion, with the strong tendency to avoid it by being dependent on others.

Aspects to the nodes give some further information on the ease or difficulty of handling the North Node task, but sign positions of the Nodes do not seem to contribute much.

The other way of using the Nodes is to look at the North Node only and its aspects and to treat it as a planet. This is the approach of the Ebertin Cosmobiology school, who give the meaning to the Node of adaptability, good fellowship, sociability and generally the way we form associations with others. It thus has a meaning rather like that of a combination of Jupiter and Saturn in its positive, 11th principle mode (or Uranus). Both sign and house position of the North Node as well as aspects seem to me to be useful for this interpretation of the Node.

I have some evidence from my own work that the nodal axis has some connection with making new departures, either in one's head or one's physical circumstances. This links to some extent with Ebertin's suggestion of adaptability. I have not done a great deal of work on this at the time of writing. It is offered as a suggestion that the reader may care to check out.

3

Aspects

I have come increasingly to the view that the *kind* of aspect between two planets is of less importance than the fact that an aspect exists. Aspects do have a nature of their own, which adds its flavor to the combination of the planets. However, I now consider that this is a matter of fine tuning and, at least as a first level of interpretation, I no longer make the conventional distinction between kinds of aspects.

One reason is that the transformational approach to the use of the information from the chart involves, *in essence*, getting beyond the dualities of the space-time world and allowing whatever is there to be there nonjudgmentally so that we are not stuck in it. This applies just as much to the apparently "good" qualities of a Venus-Jupiter trine as to the apparently "bad" qualities of a Mars-Saturn square. It is *all* part of the drama, part of the script that God comes out of the office with.

The second reason is an empirical one. It is that, in practice, the distinction between the good and bad, or hard and soft, aspects is by no means as clear as many books would have us believe. I am hardly the first to point this out. Charles Carter drew attention to it in his book on aspects years ago, and other eminent astrologers have said it since but, somehow, the myth goes on being perpetuated. I have particularly and repeatedly noticed the issue with soft aspects of Saturn. Trines and sextiles of Saturn, especially to Moon and Venus, are every bit as inhibiting and restricting as conjunctions or squares.

The difference is that the soft aspects correlate with a quality of resignation and expecting very little. People with these aspects often don't know how damaged they are. They almost always have the gift of being able to look good, and they frequently go about the world as though they have everything under control and not a care to trouble them. Barbara, in the third transcript of Chapter 9, Part I, is an example, with her Moon trine Saturn. What it seems to be is that Saturn trines and sextiles make the inhibition easier to put up with. In some ways this is actually more difficult to deal with than the hard aspects because it is more insidious. People with hard aspects of Saturn to Moon and/or Venus *know* they are unhappy and seek to do something about it, if only by complaining about their lot. People with the soft aspects either don't know they are unhappy or they know and are too embarrassed to mention it or do anything about it. Similar considerations apply to soft aspects of Neptune.

The key, I think, lies in the often repeated statement that soft aspects represent emotional configurations that are relatively inert, and hard ones configurations that are highly unstable. In the case of unpleasant emotional configurations the two types of aspect may be compared with wounds that don't hurt and wounds that do. To a superficial glance, the second type seems obviously more troublesome but the first type may involve just as severe an inhibition of emotional functioning.

On the other side of the question, a Mars-Jupiter square, for example, does not seem to me, of itself, to be any the less of a success indicator than the trine. The possessor of the square may be more likely to upset people in going for what he wants, but he may well take the view that that's their problem and be totally unconcerned about it.

Having made that point, it is definitely useful to have some knowledge of the meanings of the different kinds of aspects. There may come a point in the session where the fact that one is dealing with a trine and not a square, or whatever, is a crucial factor. But my experience is that *is* in the cut and thrust of the session, where you get to verify how the client uses the planetary energies, that the difference will be important, not in the preliminary analysis.

The distinction between hard and soft, or "inert" and "dynamic," remains a useful and valid one as long as it is used with the guidelines I have suggested. Apart from that, I find it useful to classify aspects in three groups: major aspects, powerful minor aspects and subtle minor aspects. Major aspects are the conjunction, sextile, square, trine and opposition. Powerful minor aspects are the semi-sextile, semi-square, sesquiquadrate and quincunx (or inconjunct). Subtle minor aspects are the nonagen, septile, quintile and biquintile.

The difference between the major aspects and the powerful minor aspects seems to me to reside more in the allowable orb than in the actual force of the aspect. In practice, I tend to treat all the major and powerful minor aspects in the chart as though they were the same, at the first level of interpretation.

The subtle minor aspects seem to me to have a qualitative difference from the others. For one thing, they do not appear to work equally in all charts. A certain level of self-awareness and sense of purpose seems to be the factor that brings them into play. If a person is operating below that kind of threshold the subtle minors will be dumb notes. At present, I am unsure how useful they are. I used to note them as a matter of routine, but my current feeling is that they represent very fine tuning indeed.

If we think of aspects as lines in a design of, say, a carpet, the majors are broad lines of bold color that immediately stand out, the powerful minors are thinner, more delicate lines that are still bold and clear, and the subtle minors are soft shades and elusive themes that you only notice after a careful examination of the pattern. It will be evident from the session transcripts that it is hard enough work getting the client to see the major themes of his life. I see most clients only once, or at most twice. In these cases, the information from the subtle minors is not usually appropriate. With one or two people whom I have seen several times over a period of two or three years, however, the subtle minor aspects have occasionally thrown some useful extra light. They should perhaps be noted but certainly not stressed in the preliminary analysis.

On the other hand, the powerful minors seem to me to be in great danger of being undervalued by many astrologers and astrological writers. Some otherwise good basic texts ignore them, and I have heard even very experienced astrologers say things like, "It's only a semi-square," or a semi-sextile. And the whole idea of the Moon being void of course depends on the assumption that these aspects have no power.

Maybe the same thing applies that seems to apply with the subtle minors and people need to be at a certain level of development before the powerful minors really work in their charts. If this is so, however, then most people are already operating above the threshold at which they are effective. It may have been valid to ignore these non-Ptolemaic aspects fifty or a hundred years ago, but it is not valid now and vital information can be missed by not using them. The power of the quincunx seems to be becoming more generally recognized than it was but there is still a strong feeling around in many quarters that the others are optional.

Certainly, these aspects do not have as wide an orb of influence, and I only pay attention to them when they are within an orb of 3°. For the major aspects, I use an orb of 8° except for the sextile, which gets 6°. The vexed question of how large an orb to use is really a pragmatic one and boils down to how weak an effect you are prepared to consider significant. It is, of course, very difficult to quantify these effects. I have a kind of intuitive impression that major aspects operate at more or less full strength from 0° to 5°, at medium strength from 5° to 8° and then tail off rapidly. There is a residual effect up to 10° and many excellent astrologers use such orbs routinely. The powerful minors seem to me to remain at about full strength up to 3° then tail off very rapidly up to 4° or 5°. The subtle minors appear to me to work up to 1½°–2° at the very most. As with house systems, it is largely a matter of finding out what works for you and sticking to it but being open to change as your approach to the work changes.

Of the aspects listed, the sextile, quintile, biquintile and trine may be regarded as soft. All the others are inherently challenging and energy generating.

Major Aspects

The Conjunction is a spontaneous joining of energies; the two planets act in alignment with each other like two streams merging. Whether this is easy or difficult depends on the planets. A Saturn-Mars conjunction, for example, is like mixing oil and water. Generally one may say that if the planets involved are harmonious, the conjunction represents a powerful source of readily and felicitously used energy. If the planets involved are not harmonious, the energy is still powerful but discordant. A Sun-Moon conjunction is not, as might be supposed, all that felicitous since the Moon is constantly using the sign energy to revert to the past while the Sun is using the sign energy to transcend the past. The effect is rather like an annoying echo. The basic energy of the conjunction is that of unconscious outward thrust. This means spontaneity on the one hand but a tendency to overfocusing or obsession on the other.

The Sextile represents an opportunity for the two planets to work together. It is one of the soft aspects and even with inharmonious planets will usually operate in a productive manner. Often a sextile in a chart does not seem to be particularly active and it seems to require conscious effort to get it to work. It is a resource that is there ready for the taking but it needs to be recognized. It shows qualities of being rather than action.

The Square is rather like two cars crashing into each other at a crossroads. The two planets involved are in a highly charged state of crisis and tension. It is an aspect that generates energy that must be released in some way. The energy is always powerful and always discordant, even between compatible planets. Squares provide drive in a chart; they are an aspect of dynamic energy.

The Trine represents a very easy and flowing relationship between the two planets and is one of the soft aspects. Unlike the sextile it will operate whether you pay any attention to it or not. It also shows being rather than doing. The trine is often talked and written about as though it were entirely desirable, but this needs to be taken with some reserve. It may show an undesirable state of affairs which is nevertheless fairly easy to put up with so that the person becomes unconscious of the issues and resigned to them.

The Opposition is similar to a square in that it is an aspect which generates tension and crisis, but there is a more conscious quality about the opposition. It is more like two cars meeting in a narrow lane where they cannot pass each other. There is a standoff and a need for a conscious evaluation on both sides of ways of resolving the confrontation. The opposition is therefore characterized by a need for conscious awareness of relationship.

Powerful Minor Aspects

The Semi-Sextile shows a resource which is in the process of development. It is a partnership between the two planets that is just starting to emerge. It is like a new toy that doesn't always work very well and constantly needs to be fixed. At the same time it cannot be discarded.

The Semi-Square and the Sesquiquadrate can, for most purposes, be considered together. Like the square and opposition, they indicate crises and tension but the element of direct confrontation is not yet present. It is like a relationship in which issues are building up but which are not yet being fully acknowledged. There is a feeling of uncertainty and operating without previous experience. There is much potential power in these aspects but also frustration with not knowing quite how to handle them.

The Quincunx is being increasingly treated by writers as a major aspect and it is a moot point whether it should be included under that heading. It is an aspect of strain and imbalance, as though the two planets concerned would work together except that something keeps pushing them off course. It indicates that certain assumptions and fixed ideas associated with the two planets need to be examined so that they can work more smoothly together.

Subtle Minor Aspects

The Nonagen represents a quality of something needed to be constructed by the two planets. It often seems that the faster of the two planets has some deficiency of expression and for which it needs the aid of the slower planet, but there is a reluctance to acknowledge the deficiency and accept the aid. So the nonagen often shows an area of stuckness in the person's life.

The Septile has been described as an aspect of "fate." I would rather say that it shows a constant need to push beyond one's limitations, with the particular area of limitation being shown by the faster planet and the type of push being given shown by the slower.

The Quintile has been called the aspect of talent or creativity. It is perhaps better to say that it shows the possibility of joyful self-expression of the combined functions of the two planets.

The Biquintile is very similar to the quintile, but the energy is more likely to be internalized and kept to oneself.

Understanding How Aspects Work

When I wrote the first draft of this book, I stated categorically that one should beware of using standard meanings for aspects, or indeed, any other configuration. As will be evident from earlier remarks, however, I have now considerably modified this view. It now appears to me that the use of standardized meanings is a valuable saver of time and energy. My earlier position was really an awareness of the dangers of using such standard meanings blindly. Many beginning astrologers are too liable to insist that something must be so for a client because their favorite book of delineations says that it is so.

The main provisos about using standardized meanings are that you should understand the first principles from which the delineation is derived, and that you should only present it to a client as a point for discussion, not as an established fact. The same aspect is not going to work in exactly the same way in two different charts, or even in two virtually identical charts, such as for identical twins.

In the usual case, a given aspect will itself be part of a complex of aspects, which will differ from chart to chart. Signs and house positions will also have an effect. For example, a Mercury-Jupiter square will always have the characteristics of a discordant, overloaded relationship between rational thinking and faith or optimism. This clash will be greatly intensified if Mercury is in Virgo and Jupiter is in Sagittarius, but there will be more loopholes for compromise if the placings are the other way round. The house positions will complicate matters further. It will rarely, if ever, be necessary to intepret every detail to a client. You can say something like, "Generally optimistic, inclined to take the broad view and be unconcerned with details or feels unable to handle details. A tendency to misjudgment, to see problems as bigger or smaller than they really are."

If Jupiter is in Virgo and Mercury in Pisces, there may be a love of detail such that the person gets bogged down in it. You won't really know until you have discussed it with the client. It is very likely, though, that handling details and capacity for judgment will be issues in some way. This still applies in the unlikely case of having a client one day and his identical twin the next. No actor will play Hamlet in quite the same way as another actor, and what is context for one may not be context for the other.

Also, with identical twins, there will be enough difference in the Ascendant and Midheaven for some midpoint aspects involving the angles to be different. Midpoints are beyond the scope of this book but they are a powerful source of extra information.

All these considerations are something to be held in your consciousness rather than thrown at the client. The simpler and more cogent the presentation to the client, the more effective it will be, which is why I favor reducing the information to half a dozen or so broad themes. To be a good astrological counselor you need to have as deep an understanding as possible of the basic symbols of the chart. You need to know what a Mercury-Jupiter square means without having to look it up. You need constantly to be seeking to improve your interpretational skills and learning more about astrology. But, and it's a big "but," you also need to move beyond that and become skillful in the effective *use* of the information. The chart should have done its job before your client enters the room so that your attention can be fully on making the information work for him.